Carmelite Biog

FRIAR BEYOND THE PALE

A biography of Carmelite friar Fr. Elias Lynch (1897-1967)

BY WILFRID McGREAL, O.CARM.

Saint Albert's Press
2007

First published 2007 by Saint Albert's Press.

ISBN-10: 0-904849-33-3
ISBN-13: 978-0-904849-33-2

Saint Albert's Press
Whitefriars, 35 Tanners Street,
Faversham, Kent, ME13 7JN, United Kingdom
www.carmelite.org

Edited and designed by Johan Bergström-Allen, Carmelite Projects & Publications Office, York.

Typeset by Jakub Kubů, Praha, Czech Republic.
Printed by ERMAT Praha, s.r.o., Czech Republic.
Production coordinated by Pavel Kindermann on behalf of Karmelitánské nakladatelství, s.r.o.,
Kostelní Vydří 58, 380 01 Dačice, Czech Republic, www.kna.cz.

Saint Albert's Press would like to thank the following for supplying photographs and artwork: Johan Bergström-Allen, T.O.C.; Fr. Richard Copsey, O.Carm.; the Prior and Community of The Friars, Aylesford, and Ros Duddell, Prior's Secretary; Fr. Martin Kilmurray, O.Carm.; Ruth Long, Carmelite Library & Archives at the Gort Muire Carmelite Community, Dublin; Fr. Wilfrid McGreal, O.Carm. and the Community of Whitefriars, Faversham; Jason Smith, LBIPP.

Contents

Foreword 6

Foreword by the Author 9

Introducing Elias Lynch 11

Part 1: Elias Lynch – Wicklow and Kent 13

Part 2: Letters to Cahal 123

The Carmelite Family in Britain 164

The National Shrine of Saint Jude at Faversham 166

Foreword

As Carmelites we're interested in transformation, growing more and more into the image of Jesus Christ. For years many religious orders sought to achieve this by stamping out individuality and trying to make their young novices fit a certain mould. Albeit from good motives, friaries and monasteries perhaps resembled factory production lines so that – in the words of a friar within my lifetime – 'you should be able to take a Carmelite from one place, put him in another, and no one visiting the parish or community should notice the difference'.

Thank God the majority of the Church and the Order – aided by better understanding of society and psyche – no longer intends to set Carmelites in a single mould. It is certainly not the authentic model of Carmelite formation; as Saint Teresa of Avila reminds us, the first challenge confronting the human being is to know itself.

Elias Lynch was certainly ahead of his time in celebrating the giftedness of the individual, and knew himself as a child of God, despite his failings and foibles. A member of various Carmelite communities in his life – but most especially in the Kentish parish of Faversham – Elias was able to be his own unique self, and respect those he lived with as reflections of the One God. Elias was a traditional Roman Catholic, but in the best sense of that word: not a traditionalist who clings to something that never was, but rather someone who comes to possess something of value 'handed down'. In handing tradition on to others, Elias was not afraid to take risks.

In this wonderful biography Wilfrid McGreal has traced Elias's life and shown that his formation as a friar, which began in Ireland and continued in Rome, was a life-long process nourished by his relationships with fellow friars and the wider world. Elias's unique personality was nurtured by the spirit of 'Carmel', which he regarded as unpretentious and graced with a certain freedom, being the 'least regimented' of all religious orders. As Elias wrote to

6

his confrere Fr. Cahal Gallagher, 'I am glad that we do not belong to a great overpowering and magnificent religious order where the individual is crushed by the magnificence of his own organization and his only outlet is to talk about the Order to which he belongs.'

This freedom and humility inherent to Carmel made Elias available to all people. His willingness to see others firstly as human beings – and therefore wonderfully made and loved by God – before seeing them as 'Catholic' or otherwise meant that Elias was gifted with a warmth and humanity that is still fondly remembered by the more senior brothers in Britain and Ireland.

Today the British Province of Carmelites is a flourishing and ever-evolving community of communities, open to development as the changing needs of the Church and the World become apparent. If we are able to take pride in our achievements, it is because the medieval maxim holds true: 'we are dwarves standing on the shoulders of giants'. This can be considered especially apt in the case of Elias Lynch, 'The Big Man' from County Wicklow. At his requiem the Archbishop of Southwark called Elias 'one of the giants of our day'. Along with his brothers Malachy and Kilian – the former a prior of Aylesford and the latter a Prior General of the entire Order – Elias was part of a wave of giants whose ability to read the signs of the times enabled the British Province to re-establish its roots in the twentieth century. Without Elias's practical administrative skills, harnessed to the service of the Gospel, it is doubtful that the Province would exist today.

Very importantly Wilfrid knew Elias Lynch and he is to be commended for preserving the memory of Elias' humour, wisdom, and compassion. Like his subject, Wilfrid is an imaginative, munificent and energetic man whose starting point in any dealings with another person is their innate goodness and humanity. This has enabled him to engage creatively with denominational differences and become a worthy successor to Elias Lynch as a well-respected ecumenist. As a writer and broadcaster Wilfrid has shared his love of Carmel in a way that is both accessible and engaging. Like Elias, his desire to reflect the beauty of God in humanity's creative spirit has led him to foster strong relations with a wide range of artists and writers. He has taken to heart the words of Pope John Paul II that 'The world needs heralds of the gospel who are experts in humanity'.

This biography is being published in the year that the Carmelite Family has designated as the time to mark the eighth centenary of our *Rule of Saint Albert*. In the *Rule* the first Carmelite hermits – whom Elias recalled wistfully on various occasions – are wisely advised to 'keep a tight rein on your mouths… watch your step lest your tongue give offence' (Chapter 21). It was with amusement then that I read Elias's observation about his own correspondence: 'maybe someone will read these lines in days to come and learn that keeping your big mouth shut is not the whole secret of life. There are times and even occasions, when one should keep it open; to a wide degree.'

In reading this story of one of the 'patriarchs' of our Province, I promise that you won't echo the lament of Fr. Elias: 'I have suffered from people who had nothing to say and would insist on saying it'! Elias certainly had something to say, then and now, and Wilfrid has done a marvellous job of framing The Big Man's story in Elias's own words. I am grateful to Wilfrid for this work and to Johan Bergström-Allen for seeing the work through the publication process.

Tony Lester, O.Carm.
Carmelite Provincial Office, York
20th July 2007 – Solemnity of the Prophet Elijah

Foreword by the Author

In 2005 I found myself on the brink of a radical change. After fifteen years at Aylesford Priory in Kent where I had been involved with caring for pilgrims who came to the Shrine and where for over eight years I had been prior of the Carmelite community it was time to move.

Fortunately, I was given a few months sabbatical and the Provincial asked me to go over to the community at Faversham. That meant I would remain in Kent where I had roots in ecumenical activity and the media.

During the sabbatical I began to do some research on Elias Lynch who over four decades had established and rooted Carmelite presence in the small but historical town of Faversham. Gradually, Elias came alive to me as a generous, energetic and creative person. Proud of his Irish country roots, he settled in Kent and became a prominent figure in Faversham. He was ready to be involved in every aspect of life and was ecumenical before the word was common currency. Writing in the first decade of the twenty-first century, I must admire Elias's willingness to take risks and commit himself to exciting initiatives. He was a traditional Catholic but was open to ideas and tolerant of people. Today when society seems too often paralysed by fear of terrorists, Elias lived through the World War with a certain nonchalance and was not over anxious in the face of nuclear threat. He was certain of one thing: that the Christian message could overcome Communism. What mattered was getting on with the job in hand and living his life as a Carmelite friar with the minimum of fuss, ready to be a hermit but welcoming true conviviality among the brethren. Posturing was never on his agenda, and mean-minded penitential attitudes received short shrift.

These qualities and his rich character traits have led me to try and chronicle something of Elias's life. For the most part I have let Elias speak in his own words, but family, friends and Faversham parishioners have filled in the picture. I am especially grateful to his nephew, Dr. Kilian Halpin. However,

9

I feel Elias's warmth and humanity need to be celebrated. He did have faults, he could be difficult, but he was human. He also stands for a way of living priesthood and Carmelite life that goes beyond his era. He is a reminder that we need larger-than-life characters who are not afraid to make mistakes but who are unfettered by fear and convention.

Wilfrid McGreal, O.Carm.
Whitefriars, Faversham
July 2007

Introducing Elias Lynch

The story of the Carmelite Order in Britain is one of great achievements, near extinction, and then in the last hundred years or so a renewal and new growth in diversity. In every period there have been outstanding characters.

The medieval period saw figures like John Baconthorpe, Thomas Netter and Thomas Scrope, outstanding theologians and – in the case of Scrope particularly – a zealous pastor. Carmelite friars were prominent in the Reformation; John Bale and John Bird advocates of the new ways, whilst Laurence Cooke in Doncaster was an opponent of Henry VIII. The Penal Days saw many Englishmen and women joining the Order on the Continent with attempts by the friars to re-found houses in England. However, it was the nineteenth century before the Order began to take root in Britain again with the founding of numerous convents of nuns, and figures like Herman Cohen and Benedict Zimmerman enabling the Discalced Carmelite friars to become established here.

After short-lived foundations in Wales and Yorkshire the Carmelite friars took root again in England with foundations in Kent at Sittingbourne and Faversham in 1926.

The re-founding friars came from Ireland, a province of the Order that had survived the Reformation and had already established a presence in North America and Australia.

Among the pioneers of the re-founding in England were three brothers. I would like to tell the story of one of them: Elias Lynch.

Elias, whose baptismal name was Murtagh, was a man of many parts, known as *The Big Man* and yet as often with those seen as extrovert, sensitive and reflective. His life and his interaction with family, fellow friars and people at large give a fascinating insight into the Church and Society of his day. The

11

story of the Carmelite way must be a story of people; people with their hopes, visions and fragility. They are always people of their time, and yet they have shaped our present, so it is important we keep the memory alive and tell the story.

The young Elias Lynch.

Part 1

Elias Lynch – Wicklow and Kent

Anyone arriving in Dublin by air or by sea is aware of the mountains that dominate the horizon to the south of the city. Beyond the hills lies Wicklow, a county that for the most part has changed little down the years. The valleys and hills still seem remote and the farms and villages are few and lonely. The green of the valleys and the hillsides provide a living for cattle and sheep farmers. Sadly too many of the hills have been given over to forestry projects that darken the countryside. It is hard to believe that just a few miles to the north lies the urban sprawl of Dublin. Yet here in the south west of Wicklow, in the lea of Lugnaquilla, three brothers were born in a remote farmhouse who were to have an amazing impact on the Catholic community in England and Wales and who would be seen as re-founders of the Carmelite friars in Britain.

Ballymanus is a large, austere, early eighteenth-century house near Aughrim. Originally thatched it acquired a slate roof in the nineteenth century. The house is a place of substance nestling in a valley with a good garden and acres of good land around it before the hillsides take over. The house originally belonged to the O'Byrne family and Billy O'Byrne is remembered for his part in the 1798 rebellion, the uprising that led to the Union of Ireland to Britain in 1801 which paradoxically paved the road for the beginning of the evolution of the present Republic of Ireland. Towards the end of the nineteenth century Patrick and Bridget Lynch took over the farm and house at Ballymanus, leaving their property on the Carlow-Wicklow border. With new owners Ballymanus took on a fresh lease of life as the Lynchs settled in, making it a home for a family of thirteen children, four girls and nine boys. The three boys who would become Carmelites were at the younger end of the family. One of the girls, Margaret, who was born in 1895 lived on until 1994, a person of amazing vigour. Her life bridged changes in life and technology that were quantum leaps.

The three boys who were to become Carmelite friars were Murtagh (who later took the religious name Elias) born in 1897 (†1967), William (Malachy) born in 1899 (†1972), and Edward (Kilian) who was number twelve among the children, born in 1902 (†1985). For the sake of convenience I will use the names in brackets which they received when they became Carmelites and by which they are more readily recognised.

Fr. Wilfrid McGreal with the nephews of Elias Lynch at the Lynch family home, Ballymanus near Aughrim, County Wicklow.

14

Growing up in such a large family must have given plenty of scope for challenge and an early sense of community. What was obvious in later years was that while the brothers and sisters could be frank – even blunt – with one another, there was an amazing solidarity among them and deep bonds of loyalty. Let any outsider speak ill or be negative and the ranks were closed with fierce reactions. The story is told that years later Elias criticised his brother Malachy in the presence of Brocard Taylor, an eminent Carmelite who was visiting Faversham. Dr. Taylor, as he was known, joined in the criticism only to find some while after that he was being told that perhaps he might take the next train to London!

Dr. Brocard Taylor

Life in the country in Ireland at the end of the nineteenth century was far from easy, but on the whole would have differed only slightly from country life in Britain. The worst excesses of landlordism were over and the growth of educational opportunities along with increasing religious tolerance meant that the harsh oppression of the Penal Days were past. Dublin, which was a short journey from Ballymanus, was as vibrant as any city in the United Kingdom. The hope was that Home Rule would come and that issues about property rights would be settled to enable land reform to be enacted. It was, then, a world which was to a great degree at peace with itself, with a strong sense of its history and culture. It was a rural world with its rituals and characters, a world built on trust, hard work and a closeness to nature.

Years later Elias wrote about Wicklow describing himself as 'one of the sons of the soil'. His picture of the countryside is evocative and loving: 'The county of Wicklow is like a basket of eggs. Little hills filling into one another building themselves up, until finally there is the biggest mountain in the county, Lugnaquilla. Irish hills and mountains are in a class to themselves. You can walk up and over every mountain there is. The green rushes up from the valleys where rivers flow and end in purple heather covering the upper ridges. Kindly hills sheltering the grouse and partridge; the hare, rabbit and wild goat. Lugnaquilla was more than a mountain; it was a sort of personality. It dominated the lives of farmers. They were always working at *the Lug* as they called it, to see what weather was coming.'

Elias was born into this beautiful but difficult country in 1897. His father Patrick would have been forty-eight at the time, and Bridget his mother was thirty-seven. Elias was the tenth child. Years later Elias wrote with great insight about his parents. His comments come in one of a number of unpublished letters he wrote to a confrere, Cahal Gallagher. It is likely that the letters were a means of recording memories.

My Dear Cahal,

I knew a man when I was young. He was well past middle age and broad of shoulder. He always wore Irish tweeds, brown with a fleck of red, or green or blue, and boots made by a local shoe maker.

He was tall, with mutton-chop whiskers, and that kindly tolerant smile that comes to men from long endurance. He wore a flat-topped hat, rather like Churchill, black for Sundays and grey for weekdays. He walks with a slow resolute gait of a countryman. He was a moderately successful farmer, who just got by. His wants were few, he had a lovely speaking voice, low and tolerant, and he smiled easily. He seemed to accept life as a Christian should: never expecting too much and yet content with what came. A tolerant man. He used to look at the hills in the morning, as every farmer does and tried to estimate the day. Would it bring rain or sunshine? It was the difference between saving a crop or loosing it. He took what came with the fortitude of a man of the land. He complained as every man did, but he knew that ultimately it was the will of God.

I used to see him go away in his gig behind the best horse he owned; and he never went anywhere without his stick. He was incomplete without it. He was known all over the Wicklow hills as a man to be trusted and liked. As I say, he was a tolerant man. He was my father and I was twelve when he died.

My mother was not a tolerant woman. She was small and some people said she was waspish. It was life that had made her that way. She was born to struggle. She brought up a family of nine sons and four daughters, and I do not recall that any of them are a disgrace to her name. She had a tongue. It could burn the paint off a steam roller. Everyone accepted that. A woman must have her way. It was how she was born. Plenty of endurance, and too much tongue.

In Ireland a family congregates in the kitchen. She always had an audience ready made. It was the only warm place in the house, and we lived in one of the old traditional houses of the Wicklow

17

Hills. Even a big roaring fire couldn't heat that expanse of table and cupboards because the place was both kitchen and larder; sitting-room and family theatre. She presided, and within her sphere she was supreme. She laid down the law in no uncertain way.

Letters to Cahal, 31st October 1961.

Elias was just twelve years old when his father died. It is obvious that Patrick was a great role model for him as a youngster. He admired his constancy and realised that his father was respected by all and sundry. Besides the farm Patrick Lynch was involved in the local community, delegated to superintend projects, taking on responsibilities and helping those less well-off.

Elias seemed to hold his mother as much in awe as in respect. Bringing up such a large family was taxing to say the least, and in the days before laboursaving devices the work load must have been immense. Bridget is remembered for her honest cooking, wonderful apple pies, and constant care for the men of the road who knew they would always be treated generously. She was to live to a good old age and when she died her son Malachy, who was by then Novice Master of the Irish Carmelites, was there to help her journey into eternal life.

The Lynch children would have gone to school and church at Askinagap, just a short step from Ballymanus. By the time the children were growing up the National School had been established there ensuring that the basics of education were available. The Government promised these schools in the light of the 1870 Education Act but in Ireland the downside was in evidence as the schooling was in English and this meant the loss of the use of the Irish language. However, years later Elias was to praise the foundations received there, and certainly his prose style was rugged and direct.

Annacurra Church where the Lynch family worshipped.

Writing retrospectively in 1962 Elias gives us a vision of Sunday Mass at the turn of the century. Seven Lynch boys in their boots, cottas and cassocks served Mass every Sunday in the small simple chapel that served the rural community. As Elias remarks it was amazing that three of them would become Carmelites. What caught the youthful imagination was the curate who rode over to celebrate Mass.

> When it was possible for Catholics to build places of worship in Ireland after the Penal Days they were not allowed to call them churches because that was an offence to the Elizabethan Church of Ireland. So they had to call them chapels. Some of those little chapels in the hills for far-flung farming congregations were bare in the extreme. Just four walls; two rooms leading off the back.

19

One served as a sacristy and the other as stable for the priest's horse. Four buttresses leaning against the outside walls kept the place from falling down. There was always a gallery entered by an outside stairway. Downstairs the floor was either flagged or tiled; the forms were just bare and backless. Women went to the left and men to the right. The altar was wood and Saint Patrick stood on the left with Our Lady on the right. Fourteen Stations of the Cross hung around the walls. It was closed all week; never heated on Sundays. You knelt on the bare cold floor with your knees tingling with the hardness of it.

At one time there were seven Lynchs serving on the altar. We wore clobber boots and made as much noise as a company of the Coldstream Guards. If only we had been drilled a little bit, we would have been quite terrifying. I did not know then that I would become the Financial Procurator to resurrect the old English Province of the Carmelites – dead since the Reformation. I didn't know that my brother, next in years, would become a famous friar to re-found and rebuild at Aylesford the Mother House of the Carmelites in Western Europe; and above all, I didn't ever anticipate that the youngest would become the Prior General of the Carmelites. Looking back on it I do not see a better origin for ecclesiastical preferment. Farmers ever, just like the Pope.

The priest came riding on a horse from ten miles away, saying Mass half-way on his road. In leggings and riding breeches and quite evidently a horseman. We were proud to see the priest riding a horse that everyone saw was worth £50 at a time when an Irish catholic could not own a horse worth more than £5. As our fathers said, "What he can do today, we will do tomorrow". One of the congregation always took the horse and led him to the stable at the back of the church. There the horse was watered and fed. Since the walls were not very thick, during the Mass the horse could be heard stomping on the hard cobble stones of the stable. We didn't mind the stomping at all. It was the most natural sound in the whole world to us. The priest came round to his own half of the back, the sacristy. There, Mrs. Travers, the wife of the custodian, presided. There was a fire and in winter time the priest would come to warm his hands at it, and sometimes wash them at a basin by the wall. We lads stood looking on afraid to move an eyelid.

20

The priest was terrifying. Mrs. Travers was more than that. She was quite capable of coming over and smacking our ugly faces if we made too much noise or in any way offend the sanctity of the building. Then the priest was vested, and we would all troop out to the wooden floor of the altar, and the noise was horrible.

These priests were country curates, but don't imagine that at Askinagap chapel either the Mass or the sermon was of low degree. The congregation was on occasions unique. Within the parish of Askinagap was Aughavanagh, the sometime residence of John Redmond, Chairman of the Irish Parliamentary Party of the House of Commons, and some of the finest parliamentarians in Ireland took their holidays in the Wicklow Mountains, shooting, fishing, and of course talking. We knew, or met, many of them, and it was astonishing to find that their attendance at Mass on Sunday was the high point of the day, to hear the exposition of the Gospel by the curates. Forceful, direct, homely, witty and always the strong conclusion. I heard one of the members say that he had never heard any exposition in the House of Commons comparable to the simple forceful exposition of the Gospel by these sons of the soil. Of course that made us very proud indeed. I have been many years a priest now, and can recall how those fellow countrymen of mine faced their simple congregation and got right down to facts with them. They were never afraid to make people laugh. They were never afraid to give a hard dig, and everybody knew what they were talking about; it made it better.

After Mass the curate sat down to a breakfast of two boiled eggs. That is something I never understood as a boy. Why always two boiled eggs? When I was ordained I asked one of the curates the reason for it. He said, "If you had the flavour of bacon floating down on the congregation on a wet Sunday you would empty the church in ten minutes. They would not be able to sit it out and it might give the church a name for high living." Today the priest comes on a motor cycle or in a car and the horse has gone. A new age. I would love to see a horse being ridden to Askinagap again.

The congregation was unique. Women went into church immediately on arrival; the men stood around the ditch on the far side of the road until the hand bell rang summoning them to Mass and then they made their way slowly into the cold building. But

21

of course men are a very superior race in Ireland, until they get home. In public they are superb, at home they are sometimes meek indeed. Nevertheless they still hold the right side of the Church and have their rights and responsibilities.

Carmelite News September-October 1962.
The Chapel at Askinagap.

Another memory of Sunday Mass gives insight into how religion can be perceived by the young. As a boy Elias and his contemporaries were intrigued and baffled by the reading then in use for the third Sunday of Lent. The subject of the reading was fornication and so the Sunday acquired the title 'Fornication Sunday'.

A copy of the Carmelite News from 1954.

It was a day with a feeling of doom and heavy judgement. The curate always preached a sermon on fornication. Now we lads sitting round the altar steps in our crumpled surplices were very hazy about fornication; but we did gather from the priest's remarks that it was a very fatal disease and highly contagious. In fact we had a desire not to get mixed up with it in any way.

I speak about a special solemnity because not a bonnet was raised during the whole sermon. The women sat silently with their heads bowed as if against a storm. The women on the left, the men on the right, but it seemed to affect the women more heavily. The men took it calmly enough.

Looking down the chapel I remember I could see "Long Tom Doyle's" bald head glistening in the late winter sunshine which streamed through the long windows. I knew it well because he had a wart on top and I often wondered how he used to be able to avoid knocking it with his hair comb; maybe he didn't use anything, his head in his hands, sitting it out as it were. He was 6′ 7″ tall. I don't think that Tom had a clear notion about fornication either, because I heard him say that it was prevalent among horses. Old Pat Travers from the gallery beamed down upon the general scene shrouded in his brown grey beard. The shades of "Tom the Hatter" hovered around in the darkness beneath the gallery. The Misses Heffernan sat together, not indeed for mutual protection but because that was always where they sat. It was one of the most withering Sundays of Lent.

After Mass the congregation split up, travelling North and South on foot or in horse-drawn gigs. There was a note of hilarity amongst the men who were on foot; some sly asides and some downright comment upon the state of humanity in general. The men weren't entirely discreet in the presence of us kids. Maybe they thought we were too young to understand the facts of life.

So, the years went on; we grew in wisdom and in age. It was always evident on that particular Sunday that our sisters were more than usually kind to us, it was as if they feared some awful epidemic was about to overtake us and remove us from their sight. It was a feeling that quickly evaporated and was gone in a few days. I can remember some conversation from those bygone years and I am astonished at how little moderns know about life

23

and how much we knew about life once we had attained a little maturity.

We watched our elders scatter to their lonely homesteads while we wended our ways to the whitewashed house above the singing river. God be with the days when the world was young and we were young with it.

Letters to Cahal.

Among Elias's memories of his boyhood in Wicklow are stories of eccentric farmers, of crafty deals selling animals or buying land. One old character chewing tobacco nearly killed a cock as he spat out a jet of tobacco juice knocking the bird off its perch on the half door. However, the men of the road touched his heart and were well etched on his memory. One tramp that was a frequent visitor to the family home was Mat Baron and his story has a special poignancy.

Principally I remember Mat Baron, a short man with a beard, dressed in an old frieze coat almost down to his heels. He had a stick. Not one of those sticks with a crook on it, but a straight-up stick that he grasped a few inches below its knob. He carried a big pack on his back tied up in some sort of oilskin. A bearded study in brown and black, going up hill and down dale with his eyes on the ground, as a good travelling man will. The road was more important to him than the scenery.

We used to meet him sometimes on the road as we went to or came from school, this lonely old man without a house or a home. But the peculiar thing about him was this; he was always saying his rosary aloud and to himself as a lonely man will. We kids did not believe that a man would go through his life saying his rosary. We used to hide inside the ditches and listen to him as he passed by. If he knew that we were there or not, we did not care. We were slightly afraid of him although we knew that perhaps a little time later we would find him at our house. He did not seem interested in the world. His sole purpose in life seemed to be wrapped up in going on. He never imposed. He never stopped in one house more than one night. He was like the pilgrims of old. In the late evening we would find him sitting on the hob by the peat fire, sometimes mending with needle and thread the buttons that had gone adrift on his old frieze coat, and always you could hear the rosary beads near his hand.

Food is good and plentiful in the mountains; but it is rough. Good bread, good butter, good buttermilk and fat bacon – what more could a man want? People go to bed early, and the warmest place in the house is the hearth stone in front of the big fire. Our fire was a big one, maybe seven feet wide. Three fires under three pots boiling for pigs and poultry and whatever it was in the farmyard that had to be fed in the morning. Sometimes I have seen him come in with frost on his beard, covered in snow, and then he would go to his place on the hob beside the fire and dry himself out. Stretched out on the warm hearthstone at night he was warmer than we were upstairs. He was always up at cockcrow.

There was a mystery about him. None ever saw the inside of the pack he carried on his back; and one time my mother suggested to him that it was rumoured around the countryside that he had a monkey in it. Then there was an "earthquake". Old Mat went down on his hands and knees in front of us all and protested that he had nothing but what he stood up in, that he was a poor man – not merely in the things of life, but poor in hope for the future. I cannot remember the terms of his indignant protest, but I do remember the words with which he ended it up. It was a protest against those who would take the little he had away from him – even his pack.

"To whom that hath, it shall be given; and to whom that hath not, it shall be taken away, even that which he hath."

I have never seen my mother so frightened in all her life, because she seemed to hear the voice of an old prophet. It is interesting to recall that she was kinder to him after that, kinder than ever she had been to him before.

There was another time when she suggested to him that he was getting too old for the road and that he ought to go into a public institution so that he could be looked after for the rest of his days. That was the suggestion of a practical woman and it

25

was made in all kindness of heart because I often heard her say that one day the old man would be found dead in a ditch and to her it seemed that a man who would die without the Sacraments, with no one to witness his passing, was not the way a Christian man should die. She had never read the life of Paul the first hermit, and how could she understand that God's Providence will always look after God's own. And how could a good woman understand that a man who was not a farmer could be anything else. Farmers she knew, shopkeepers she knew, priests she knew, but a man without a home seemed lost to her and the workhouse seemed a better place.

The years went by and there was little change in old Mat. His rounds became a little shorter, his gait a little slower, and the pack seemed to grow bigger as he bent his face nearer to the ground. He was more silent too, if that was possible; and he seemed to turn a little more fully to the fire as he sat on the hob. But he came and went.

Then one morning a man going to the fair with a creel of young pigs, saw old Mat's camp beside a turf clamp that showed up black in the morning light, on top of the hill that looks down on Greenane. There was something about his outstretched arm that called for help, so he climbed down and went over to see him. Yes, the old man was in bad shape. The farmer called to the priest's house and told the priest. So it was that on a late summer morning, on the bare hilltop, surrounded by the heather and the turf, the old man received his last Holy Communion. He died later on in the morning. His pilgrimage was over.

You may know the Wicklow Hills – not those harsh, rugged disturbances pitted with rock and crowned with snow and ice that you see in Switzerland, but hills that flow softly like the breasts of Kathleen Ni Houlihan. The kindest hills in all the world. Some of them run green right up to the top and down the other side. Then you meet the hills where the green runs into bracken, and the bracken runs into heather, where the partridge calls. There is, or used to be, a rabbit in every furze bush; and where you meet the bog, the black cock calls. I wish I could hear again the drumming of the jacksnipe, just when the night is falling down on the world and the bees are going home. It is on the top of the hills that you find the turf.

Men go up in the summer time and dig it out with slanes and let it dry. Then they foot it and clamp it, so that the wind blows through it. Then down it comes on sleds to provide fuel for the winter. If there is one memory an Irishman carries with him wherever he goes it is the smell of the turf fire. You get the tang of it over every bog. These turf clamps are one of the most familiar sights in Ireland, and turf cutting and turf harvesting always partakes of something like a picnic. It is a day in the bogs. It was on the shady side of one of these black clamps that Mat Baron laid himself down for the last time.

Well, the doctor came and it was decided not to have an inquest because the man had died of old age. Still dressed in his frieze coat they laid him upon a turf sled and lined it with heather. They made him a rough coffin and painted a cross on it with the red raddle used for marking sheep. Some good woman produced a crucifix instead. They opened his pack, and it was then they found the real nature of the man.

He was an old Carmelite lay–brother from one of the houses in the West of Ireland that had fallen into decay. Finally at the end of the Penal Days, the Community – a Prior and one lay-brother – had dispersed and gone upon their separate ways. In the pack they found his old habit. It was not the Third Order habit that we usually know among the Tertiaries. It was a full and well worn old habit, greasy and a little dirty and he had carried it with him ever since he had been on the road.

These good people knew what a religious habit was, so they stripped him of his old frieze coat and clothed him in his habit. Then, beneath the old coat they found a crucifix on a long chain. Someone noticed that behind the body on the cross was a paper. A paper wrapped on oiled silk, and on it was written Mat Baron's Vow:

27

"To walk Thy roads until I die,
     in hunger, cold and sunshine
To see Thy cross on every hill,
     In the branches of every tree
To see Thy blood upon the stones,
     Of every lane and roadway
And bring my soul to God above,
     By my Lady's rosary."

A Carmelite had gone back to the hermit's life and had ended his journey like Paul the Hermit.

Carmelite News Christmas 1955. Tramps Mat Baron.

The death of the head of the family in 1909 on Boxing Day would have been a moment of crisis. Some of the family was already in Dublin establishing business connections that were to flourish. So before long Elias made the transition from Wicklow to Dublin, not a great distance, but in those pre-1914 days there would have been an immense culture shock. Dublin like any city was a place of contrasts. It had its imposing Georgian squares, affluent suburbs and the beauty of the coast leading out to Bray. It was also a busy port. There was a large British military presence and more than a share of poverty with the attendant ills. Elias was fascinated by the city but he felt he was living in some way on the wrong side of the track. The Grand Canal flowing under Portobello Bridge divided the posh suburbs of Rathmines and Rathgar from areas like the Coombe.

The Coombe, centred round Saint Patrick's Cathedral, was perhaps the dingiest part of the city with a flavour all of its own. It had almost its own separate language. It was broad and deliciously vulgar. Some of the flavour of it comes out in that old Dublin ditty *Billy Mulligan the pride of Coombe*. Today most of it has been swept away under the cleansing influence of Guinness' Brewery.

28

Elias remembers the shops selling spare ribs, pigs' heads and trotters, and he relished the memory of suppers of cabbage and pig's cheeks. The children of the area were full of mischief, with the girls as brash as the boys.

They had a vocabulary unequalled by any brand of infant produced in the metropolis but their hearts were pure gold. They were the cockneys of Dublin and some of their unique character came down to them from the old Danish settlers in Dublin.

Besides the kids there were the cobblers sitting in their windows to catch the light, not just mending but making shoes of pure leather. The medical hall housed the apothecary with his yellow and green symbols. He made medicine with his pestle and mortar pounding to dust the ingredients that would restore health.

Dublin also offered the young man from the country wonders like the cinema; though silent moving pictures were still a novelty they were a great draw in a city that loved drama. The Dublin trams driven by Wicklow men also stick in his memory; cumbersome vehicles but all part of a new life.

Not far from the Portobello Bridge the great dividing line for Elias was the Portobello Barracks, home to various regiments of the British army. Years later Elias recalls his memories of these soldiers; their forays into Dublin life and their love of pigs' cheeks and trotters.

> Portobello Bridge is long in my memory. You see, it was a canal bridge with a hump on it and the trams used to rattle up and over it like a horse that is clearing a hurdle. About a mile up the canal was Portobello Barracks – it was not spectacular to look at, just that dreary parade-ground in the centre with a sentry at the gate, sergeant majors shouting their heads off and poor infantry men stamping their way over the hard ground. It was just about a half-mile upstream from Portobello Bridge and the banks of the canal were unlighted at that time. The soldiers were always

29

allowed free on Saturday nights but they had to be in by eleven. I seem to remember names of famous regiments – The King's Own Scottish Borderers, the Sherwood Foresters – but maybe these are names that come to me from out of the air, I cannot really remember whether they were or not. These young fellows, Scottish or English, used to walk home to barracks up Richmond Hill, sharp right at the canal, swagger sticks under their left arm; those swagger sticks were really things to be coveted – short little canes not more than 18" or 2' long with a round knob indented with a crest of the regiment. They stuck those swagger canes under their armpit, swung their arms and always in twos made their way home, liberally lubricated with Guinness. At the lower end of Richmond Street there was a shop that specialised in pigs' trotters; these came salted in barrels from Denmark. It was usual to break open the top of the barrel and turn the tap on so that the soft Dublin water rinsed the salt away, then on Saturday the whole barrel full was boiled and turned out steaming in the window just when the soldier boys were on their way home. Each bought a pair of trotters steaming hot; they had to be wrapped in greaseproof paper and then they were wrapped in a red paper. In that way a soldier could tuck his pair of pigs' trotters beneath his arm and hold his swagger cane in position with his left hand and you would need to look closely before you could see the parcel. Then, the minute they turned up the darkened banks of the canal they started to eat the trotters. The bare bones went into the canal and I dare say in that stretch of water you could find more eels than in any other part of the canal system. By the time they got to the barrack gate they were ready to turn in.

One must remember that those lads were in a foreign country. They had their own pubs which they frequented in the city and there was a special character to their ruddy red faces, but they marched without looking either to the left or the right; they greeted nobody; they went their way, but they had their friends.

I knew a sergeant once in charge of the privates' mess and their idea of a party corresponded so closely to my own that I sometimes felt tempted to join the army. I am talking of nearly sixty years ago before the days of the new pig. Those were the days of the large porker, and much of the meat went into pork sausage and other combinations of minced meat. The pork butcher used to slip his knife beneath the rib cage and with a few deft strokes off would come the whole rib system like a lady's corset. Of course the meat was salted and smoked – sometimes these spare ribs as they were called came in from Denmark, always salted to cure them, but without brine because otherwise they would be paying freight on water. These spare ribs were boiled with cabbage, but the cabbage wasn't split up into leaves, it was boiled in the round and then cut into sections, and that was one of the things that sometimes the men craved for and it would be the duty of the Mess Sergeant to go out and buy them. Sometimes he bought a whole barrel full of spare ribs and it was not surprising to see a farmer's cart from around Templelogue pulling in at the barrack gate with a big load of small Savoy cabbages.

Now I am afraid that these days are all gone in Dublin; we have become far too nice; our manners have improved so much we hardly know ourselves, but I could still tell if there are spare ribs and cabbage passing the front door of a house. How often do I remember smells and flavours of my youth – I never seem to forget and yet I am unable to recover them.

Letters to Cahal.

Memories of years gone by. The throw-away remark about thinking of joining the Army is poignant because Elias would have been old enough by then to join but if he had then he would have been caught up into the killing-fields of Flanders.

Like any young person Elias wanted to make something of his life and it is not surprising that the army with its sense of camaraderie should have appealed to his warm outgoing personality. His office job was obviously not enough and so he was open to suggestions. He was aware that while educated in the basics he needed to develop academically, yet he realised what he had to offer was himself. The notion of a calling to the priesthood came as something of a challenge from friends he had got to know in Dublin. They asked "Why

31

don't you become a missionary?" and with that question something stirred in Elias. He realised he had to do something about the future. Not long before he died he wrote about a momentous Saturday evening in his youth that was to change his life.

I am a late vocation. I was working in Dublin in a very unimportant office, but I was a Wicklow man and consequently was in touch with Wicklow men who have a certain community interest. It is a short walk from the Wicklow Hills to a job in Dublin.

One of my friends at the time was a Chief Superintendent of the Dublin Metropolitan Police. One of his sons, called Matt, was a student of All Hallows College. This is a Missionary College. The Chief Superintendent lived in Dublin Castle, in a house provided by the Administration. I used to go there occasionally in my free time for a cup of tea and one day Matt said to me, "Why don't you try to become a Missionary?" It was an idea that had never entered my head but I thought about it and in subsequent meetings I talked to him about it, and finally I went one evening to see the head of a missionary congregation. He was out. I waited an hour, and since I have never waited an hour for any man – I walked out. It is a bad idea.

You have to remember how little I had to offer besides myself. I had an elementary education, which meant I could write as well as a scribe, and spell as well as a university professor, and nothing more. These two virtues have remained with me through my life. Now I cannot write so well, but I can still spell. For many years I have tried to teach my secretary the secret of spelling, punctuation and the rest of it.

I was living in Baggot Street, Dublin. I was free on Saturday evening after six o'clock and, because I had been reared in piety, I used to go to confession at the University Church in Stephen's Green. There was a very fine confessor there who was very popular amongst the elite. I was not part of that. This Saturday night I went in and found about thirty people waiting for confession in rows of seats. I knelt at the back and as the clock passed nine I decided that hope of confessions had finished. I came out into the porch and stood undecided. Then a man came up to me and said, "I am going over to Whitefriars Street. They hear confessions there until the line is finished." So, with him, I walked to old Whitefriars Street. Today the church has been modernised out of all comparison. I knew the place well. There was one box occupied by an old priest educated in Louvain who would not let you call him "Father". He insisted upon being called "Mister". He used to retort to people who called him "Father", "I'm not your father." It was of course, the old French custom coming down from the Penal Days when Irish students were educated in Louvain and were known as "Monsieur l'Abbé." The Italian custom of "Father" had not been accepted by these men as universal. I have a certain sympathy with them.

So I found myself in the old Whitefriars Street Church, kneeling fourth, or fifth in line. When it came to my turn it was ten o'clock and as I pulled the door of the confessional, out came a bearded friar, tall in his magnificence. He passed me by as if he had not seen me. I was left standing in some puzzlement and then I ducked into the next confessional which was still open for business. By accident, or by design of God, I found myself going to confession to Father John Cogan, the Provincial of the Irish Carmelites. He was, perhaps, the only priest in all of Dublin who could have solved my problem, or would even have taken an interest in it.

I didn't have much to confess. I was more troubled about the future than the past, and I asked this priest to tell me what to do. I knew by his attitude that I was his last patient because he spent a little more time with me than upon the women who wanted to tell how they lost their tempers with their husbands, or with the children.

He said to me, "You may have a vocation to the religious life. We have no time to go into it now, but will you go out to Terenure College and have a talk with Father John Maganetty and he will sort you out?" I made a telephone appointment.

I had just graduated to a bowler hat and a belted raincoat. I went out to Terenure College and walked up the drive to find a white gate guarding the sacred precincts of the College from ambitious cows. Leaning on the gateway was a bearded friar in Carmelite habit resting his arms upon the top bar. He made no attempt to open the gate to me. I said to him, "I have come to see

33

Father John Maganetty." He looked at my bowler hat and belted raincoat and said, "Are you home on furlough?" He opened the gate and let me in. I was about to see a man who became in later years one of the major inconveniences of my life. He asked me what I knew. He found that I knew very little. I didn't know the difference between the dative and ablative in the Latin declension. He decided to take me. Why, I do not know.

For two years I worked in dumb obedience to a text book until I finally matriculated to the National University. My memory was terrible. My power of concentration poor; but I did possess a certain power of improvisation. That saved me. After a year at the National University, undistinguished by any record, the Superior of the Carmelite Order, reared and matured in the classical tradition, decided that the only thing to do with us was to send us all off to Rome in the hope that Roman education, Roman tradition, would turn us into civilised Europeans and even acceptable Carmelites. I have been glad of that ever since.

If you want to find out what happened to me when I went to Rome read a little letter in a previous edition of the *Carmelite News* called "The Mouse of San Martino."

I have often recalled the anonymous man who spoke a few casual words to me in the porch of the University Church, Stephen's Green, Dublin. I remember we paused for a moment opposite York Street to decide whether we would go to Clarendon Street or Whitefriars Street, both of them Carmelite Churches, one Calced and the other Discalced. We decided in favour of Whitefriars Street because, in the words of my friend, "They are not so holy over there." We entered the church and went our different ways; I to be a Carmelite, and he to go home to his wife. He didn't know, and nor did I, that our casual encounter that night made three men Carmelites, because my two brothers followed me into the Order; one of them was to become its Prior General.

What a thought it is! How a casual encounter in the porch of a church can start a reaction that will change the lives of three men, who in struggle and strife will one day arrive at the priesthood. I had no idea that joining the Carmelites was only just a little worse than joining the French Foreign Legion.

Carmelite News May 1964. Late Vocations.

Fr. John Stanislaus Megannety

Fr. John Stanislaus Megannety (front left) in Avoca, the area where Elias Lynch grew up.
Others shown here during the Silver Jubilee of Fr. Cogan are (left-right) Fr. McCabe,
Fr. R. Walsh, Mrs. Hickey, Fr. Griffin and Fr. Colfer.

35

The throwaway line "joining the Carmelites was only just a little worse than joining the French Foreign Legion" perhaps had some truth when we hear something of the rigours of life for a young Carmelite in the early years of the twentieth century.

Years later Elias was to call the Carmelites the least regimented of all orders, but in the early part of the twentieth century the Order like many other religious families was suffering from the after-effects of the upheaval of Europe in the nineteenth century and anti-clericalism. By the beginning of the twentieth century the Carmelite friars in Ireland could be aware that despite relatively small numbers they were active and reaching out with new ventures in New York and Australia. Their presence in Dublin was well established and Dr. Spratt had been a focus of energy with the works for the poor that he initiated from Whitefriars Street in the mid-nineteenth century.

However, in the years just before the outbreak of the First World War a certain rigour was introduced into the day-to-day living of the friars which came partially from the Church climate of the day and the zeal of the Prior Provincial, Father Southwell. Added to that, Roman superiors had the school at Terenure closed, being seen as an inappropriate apostolate. Despite the negatives, Dublin folk had a special love for the friars and among their numbers were individuals who would reinvigorate the Order in Ireland and influence a new generation. Among these was Elias Magennis and John Cogan. The former would prove to be a most effective Prior General, while John Cogan would give sensitive leadership to the Order in Ireland. Both were to be key figures in supporting the re-founding of the Order in Britain offering their support and leadership. Elias's early years in the Order correspond to the years when the struggle for Irish independence was at its height. A number of Carmelites in Dublin and New York including Elias Magennis were fervent supporters of the struggle. Whitefriars Street was only a stone's throw from Stephen's Green and the Post Office, scenes of the Easter Rising. However,

Fr. Peter Elias Magennis

Fr. John Cogan

while some members of his family were caught up in the Troubles, Elias – who was always proud of his roots – never seems to have been involved in the world of nationalism.

Elias does leave us with some references to his early days in the Order, painting pictures of a certain austerity which he bore with reluctance. His reluctance was rooted in an awareness that young friars were treated without sufficient care for their health and welfare. Certainly in later life he always ensured that those he lived with never lacked good food and proper support.

37

Whitefriars Street Carmelite Church in Dublin today.

Elias has left us with a picture of his early years in the Order after his time as a novice at Terenure in the southern suburbs of Dublin.

> The years went on and I became a seminary student in the Carmelites four miles out upon the right side of the track. I became a novice in the Carmelites; then I was professed; then I matriculated at the National University and of course I had to attend lectures at the University every day – sometimes in the morning and sometimes in the afternoon and one had to eat in between. The only way that that could be done was to walk back the four to five miles between the University and Terenure College to pick up enough energy to walk back again. Sometimes it meant walking the best part of twenty miles a day. I have stated somewhere in my memoirs that joining the Carmelites at that

38

Terenure College in September or October 1914.

time was like joining the Foreign Legion. The Foreign legion had the advantage that they wore boots and socks; they wore heavy coats in the heat to keep the sun out, but when they arrived at barracks they had wine, women and song. We students started the day upon porridge, skimmed milk, shell cocoa, bread and margarine, and from there on we faced the day. It never occurred to any Superior of the Carmelites in those days that it was four to five miles from the College to the University, but you had to get there and back again, maybe twice a day. Many of my fellow students had bicycles – I had a bicycle too, but I learned that out of consideration for the public I had better walk. One day when I went by bicycle I ran broadside on to a car and ended up sitting on the bonnet. It wasn't nice.

However, I got through the Arts course, but all my reactions were those of a country lad. One day I walked over the hump of

39

Portobello Bridge; on the right-hand side of the street there were a greengrocer's and butcher's side-by-side just beside where the tram cars used to stop. The greengrocer displayed his potatoes in trays in the open and as I walked by, out from the butcher's shop ran a mongrel dog carrying in his mouth a large steak; my reactions were immediate, I picked up a potato from the open tray and threw it at the dog. It caught him right behind the ear and he dropped the steak and ran yelping away. Then I found that the tram driver had been a witness to the incident. He leaned out of his cab and clapped me right heartily. The butcher crossed the street and retrieved his steak – what he did with it I never enquired, but I don't suppose that dog ever tried to steal another steak from that butcher's shop.

Then, somehow or other, the story got around and the drivers who were Wicklow men welcomed me on board their trams. Of course there were inspectors and occasionally they got on, but the conductor would come along and give me a ticket, which he had to account for at the end of his journey. This troubled my conscience. My brother Jim lived a short way up the canal and I told him this story so he went and got four five-shilling bags of copper and said, "Give that to the man in charge at the terminus and whenever you are short of a ticket they can take the money from that." Well, it seemed to me that that pound in copper lasted a long time, but I never walked again if I could help it, that stretch of straight road from Terenure to Harcourt Street Station. It made a big difference to me. Can you imagine it? It never occurred to our venerable superiors to give even one of us our tram fare when the weather turned to rain or snow.

Trams and Terenure

40

The incident with the bicycle says something about Elias for while he was physically big he never felt totally at ease with his body, sensing an awkwardness. In later years he could seem big and fierce but it was an exterior that belied a gentleness and a vulnerability.

The old cliché of 'out of the frying pan into the fire' applied to the next stage in Elias's Carmelite formation. He was sent to Rome along with a small group of his contemporaries, one of whom being his younger brother Malachy [William] who had followed him into the Order. They were both professed as Carmelites in 1918 and were to spend six years in Rome until their ordination in 1925.

Malachy Lynch, brother of Elias and Parish Priest in Faversham 1927-29.

41

Writing in 1961 Elias gives his picture of that period. Most of the time was spent in the old Carmelite Priory of Saint Martin (San Martino ai Monti) which was near the Basilica of Saint Mary Major, while the latter part was spent at the International Study Centre of Saint Albert (Sant'Alberto) close by Castel Sant'Angelo and the Tiber. Writing in 1961 he gives a vivid picture of those days.

> I was nineteen before I started to learn Latin. I had a bad memory and it was a terrible task. Eventually I matriculated to the National University of Dublin and after a few years my Superiors decided that our class was very poor material, and that higher education was a waste of money. At that time there was a line of Superiors in the Province who were right out of the top drawer in academic qualifications. They looked upon our generation as being just the run of the mill. Life has since taught them some lessons, but many of them died without repenting their errors. They yanked us out of the University and drafted us into what they proudly called the Collegio di San Martino ai Monti in Rome. We were a new growth in that place. Mushrooms in an old shed.
>
> San Martino was an old Carmelite convent belonging to the Roman Province, mostly unused, and we settled down under a Maltese Superior, a delightful old boy, strict but kindly, and he liked the Irish. We learned as time went on that his occasional explosions of temperament were just a national characteristic. We were only a dozen or so, and of no importance whatsoever.
>
> There was a great big 'sala' or room framed with pictures of old Carmelite saints, all numbered because they were, as was the convent, the property of the Italian Government. That august body had confiscated all religious property on the formation of United Italy. Those who know Italy may recall that a United Italy is a fantasy of nationalistic imagination. However that is only a part of the story. Even the chairs and settees around the walls belonged to the Government, as did indeed the very tiles upon which we walked. There was a small kitchen, a makeshift oratory, a few single rooms for the Prior and senior students. The

rest of us were bedded down in a large room divided by curtains into cubicles. The cubicles were roomy, I admit. There was a very large window at one end and a very small top window at the other. There was plenty of light and of course the climate was hot enough for Africans. Each of us had our cubicle and that was the only privacy we had. There was a small bedside table and a few hooks on which to hang our habits. Beds were old iron bedsteads boarded with wood on which lay a straw mattress. There was no intention of turning into guardsmen but those beds certainly did give us straight backs, and very often a certain soreness where soreness is not appreciated amongst students who must sit for the waking hours of the day on hard benches and unyielding choir stalls. It was a hard life but we were young and prepared for anything. I still look back and wonder how on earth we endured it.

Looking down into the garden of San Martino the big crickets used to rub their legs all day in the trees creating the cricket noise. We didn't like them very much, because they were the same colour as the leaves and one is not interested in what one cannot see. On our beds in the cubicles we had sheets and a blanket and a bolster as hard as wood. I had the end cubicle. Sometimes I lay there sweating out the Roman day. I noticed a hole in the corner of the wainscoting and if you remained quiet, out used to come a little mouse. First his head and whiskers – and what magnificent whiskers they were. Beautiful! Surely three inches wide. There he used to sit halfway out of the hole looking at me. Then I began to leave a little of the mousetrap cheese on which we were fed and a crust of bread outside the hole. Sure enough he took it, and then I began to love mice. This graceful little chap used to raise the small chunk of cheese in his two pink paws and eat it up. Bread he didn't much care for, but eventually it used to disappear. In that end cubicle he and I were like Saint Jerome and the lion. He did love cheese. Also he had a sense of time. He knew exactly when the cheese should appear and evidently expected it. He was not afraid. He was just like a little man sitting on a fence.

One day I forgot the cheese, because instead of the yellow hard cheese the Prior decided to give us nice cream cheese so I ate the lot and there was nothing left for the mouse. I lay down on the hard bed for the siesta and went half asleep. Suddenly I wakened,

43

and there was Mr. Mouse sitting on the bolster beside my head as much as to say, "What has happened to you? Where is my cheese?" There was nothing I could do about it except to promise him that next day he would have a double portion. We became very friendly. I loved his whiskers and his clean pink paws. He was a little gentleman. In the end I used to find him sitting on my bolster when I came home and he would not stir. Sometimes at night I used to feel him scrambling around the bed. He was becoming very friendly indeed. One evening as he sat on the little ledge I saw another whisker behind him. I thought, "Now you have got a wife." But that was not the end of it. In about ten days out came five little chaps just like father and mother and then the cheese became quite a problem. I had to confide in other students, but I found that there was a great divergence of opinion on mice. The whole difficulty was solved because eventually the student body of San Martino was moved to Sant'Alberto and the Italian mice of San Martino were left to find another patron.

At San Martino we were up and about at five in the morning. Then we had a half-hour's meditation in choir. At least that was the intention, but I am afraid that many of us went to sleep. Don't regard that as lack of piety, it was just that we were students from the soft humid green Isle of Erin and the Roman heat sucked our very lives away. Not that anybody noticed it in the least. Roman Superiors are the most hard-hearted category of men in the whole wide world.

After meditation we had morning hours. After a quick breakfast of coffee and rolls with butter of a very suspicious character we set out upon a four mile walk to the Collegio di Sant'Alberto down the verges of Saint Peter's. There we spent the morning and afternoon before we returned home. They were trying to make us philosophers and theologians.

I well remember the morning's journey and equally well the return in the afternoon. We always went the same road. We got to know every inch of it. We knew the smell of every shop we passed. We began to know even the people who lived and worked in the streets. We were a class apart from them. They paid little attention to us but <u>we noticed them</u>. How I remember the cobble stones! How I remember the steps we climbed down in the morning and

44

climbed up in the afternoon. How I still remember the smells and the stinks of the Roman back streets.

This is what we saw in the morning. We climbed the cobbles of an ascending street and then down about thirty steps to drop into a by-street before we came out on the main avenue. Tenement flats seven storeys high on each side mercifully shaded us from the morning sun. There was the stink of every human, animal and vegetable. We passed under a canopy of washing hung out from the windows above. Some of those washing lines extended to about eight feet over the street. They had most ingenious ways of pulling out and pulling in the washing and of seeing that things didn't drop off. Every kind of male and female garment fluttered in the wind and became dry in the hot Italian sun. Laundry was not a question of drying; it was just a question of washing. In those tenements hundreds of people lived; kindly and talkative. In them they were born, lived and died. They were not concerned with us and we were not concerned with them.

But there was Neddy. Neddy was the scruffiest donkey you ever saw. He belonged to a charcoal burner. His job was to carry in the panniers on each side of his back a load of wood to a backyard where his master burned it to make charcoal.

You must remember that Roman women did not use gas or electricity or coal to prepare their meals, they used charcoal. There is no elaborate kitchen equipment. There is just a pan with a number of holes to give air when the charcoal is lit. Over the charcoal pans, meals simple and elaborate were prepared. Have you ever tasted a steak prepared over a charcoal fire? When it is just hot and frizzling they spread a mixture of Italian cheese and butter over it with a little salt or pepper. Never forget the chip potatoes. In France they call it Chateaubriand steak. It is served on a twelve inch plate. Dinner starts with a generous plate of macaroni or spaghetti dusted with cheese and then follows the steak and chips. When an Italian gets that under his belt he is at peace with his wife and therefore the world for the next two days. This is to show how important charcoal is, because there is nothing to replace charcoal in cooking. It is hot, yet it is slow and it gives that inimitable flavour to steak that no other method of cooking gives. I have often wondered what a revolution would

45

come about in Ireland if wives could provide their husbands with food like that. How happy men would be!

But we must return to Neddy. He had the longest ears of any ass I ever saw, but he wasn't interested in us. Why should he be? We were just about as interesting as a procession of ducks. Neddy had his rights in that street. He had established them by long and painful endeavour and he preserved them by the force of his two hind legs which could teach a lesson to anyone who intruded on his territory.

In that narrow street of Roman tenements the ash can is the recipient of everything that is thrown away. Into it went ashes, broken plates, cabbage leaves and the residue from every kind of vegetable from the Roman markets. Lettuces, artichokes, onion tops, in fact the lot. Neddy had a way of teaching manners to people. In time the housewives learned that all residue in bread and vegetables should be placed neatly on top of the ash cans because if they were not Neddy would knock the ash cans over and spread the contents over the street. The resulting war with the dustmen was not a subject for poetry.

Roman students walk in crocodile two by two, like the animals going into Noah's ark. We used to go down through that noisy, roaring tunnel between the Quirinale Palace to the Piazza d'Espagne, past the statue of the Immaculate Conception, over the bridge of the Tiber to our academic day in the Collegio di Sant'Alberto. Sweating in the hot Italian morning sun, footsore and tired, to commence a day that would have horrified any university student of modern days. Let no-one ever tell me that the life of a student in Rome is a picnic. It is more like Devil's Island.

We started home about five o'clock in the evening and we tried to avoid the crowded streets and go through the lanes. There was more shade. In the narrow lanes the broad-minded ladies of the Roman scene congregated to catch the eye of passers-by. We walked past them with eyes ahead like Her Majesty's Brigade of Guards, but we had to bear the barrage of comment that came forth from the four corners of the lanes. I cannot tell you what they used to say, I can only indicate it. We were a normally good-looking lot of young fellows in the twenties; tall, athletic, and of course

46

dedicated to the higher life. We carried our books under our arms or hung in a satchel from our shoulders. The general substance of their remarks was that we represented a terrible waste of <u>good human material</u>; that, in fact, we had fallen into the wrong hands. They had their likes and dislikes among us but there was one who excelled beyond all others in their preferment; a handsome young redhead from County Tipperary. They couldn't understand why it was that such a handsome fellow could find himself marching

WHITEFRIARS
FAVERSHAM
KENT

The Carmelite News

DECEMBER, 1961 —
JANUARY, 1962
NUMBER

Published by the St. Mary's College Building & Missionary Fund

THE MOUSE OF SAN MARTINO

I was nineteen before I started to learn Latin. I had a bad memory and it was a terrible task. Eventually I matriculated to the National University of Dublin and after a few years my Superiors decided that our class was very poor material, and that higher education was a waste of money. At that time there was a line of Superiors in the Province who were right out of the top drawer in academic qualifications. They looked upon our generation as being just the run of the mill. Life has since taught them some lessons, but many of them died without repenting their errors. They yanked us out of the University and drafted us into what they proudly called the Collegio de San Martino ai Monti, in Rome. We were a new growth in that place. Mushrooms in an old shed.

San Martino was an old Carmelite convent belonging to the Roman Province, mostly unused, and we settled down under a Maltese Superior, a delightful old boy. Strict, but kindly, and he liked the Irish. We learned as time went on that his occasional explosions of temperament were just a national characteristic. We were only a dozen or so, and of no importance whatsoever.

A great big sala or room, framed with pictures of old Carmelite Saints, all numbered, because they were, as was the convent, the property of the Italian Government. That august body had confiscated all religious property on the formation of United Italy. Those who know Italy may recall that a United Italy is a fantasy of nationalistic imagination. However, that is only a part of the story. Even the

chairs and settees around the walls belonged to the Government, as did indeed the very tiles upon which we walked. There was a small kitchen, a make shift oratory, a few single rooms for the Prior and the senior students. The rest of us were bedded down in a large room divided by curtains into cubicles. The cubicles were roomy, I admit. There was a very large window at one end and a very small top window at the other. There was plenty of light and of course the climate was hot enough for Africans. Each of us had our cubicle and that was the only privacy we had. There was a small bedside table and a few hooks on which to hang our habits. Beds were old iron bedsteads boarded with wood on which lay a straw mattress. There was no intention of turning us into guardsmen but those beds certainly did give us straight backs, and very often a certain soreness where soreness is not appreciated amongst students who must sit for the waking hours of the day on hard benches and unyielding choir stalls. It was a hard life but we were young and prepared for anything. I still look back and wonder how on earth we endured it.

Looking down into the garden of San Martino the big crickets used to rub their legs all day in the trees creating the cricket noise. We didn't like them very much, because they were the same colour as the leaves and one is not interested in what one cannot see. On our beds in the cubicles we had sheets and a blanket and a bolster as hard as wood. I had the end cubicle. Sometimes as I lay there sweating out the Roman day, I noticed a hole in the corner of the

The story of the Mouse of San Martino as it originally appeared in The Carmelite News.

47

in a crocodile of dedicated celibates. They didn't know that we understood Italian and of course they didn't understand English; but we had fun.

One day we met the Parish Priest of that district because our choir was invited to a function in his church. We told him about our experiences in the lanes. He told us that these women were the most generous donors to Saint Anthony's Bread in the whole parish; that although they would not officially have anything to do with him their charity towards the poor was boundless. His comment was, "There is good in everybody." Much water has flowed under the bridges of the Tiber in the forty years that divide us from then. Life has taught me also that there is much good in even the worst of us.

Carmelite News December 1961. The Mouse of San Martino.

While the years in Rome had their downsides it must have been exciting and exhilarating to be in a city with such history and art. It was also – as in Ireland – a time of upheaval as the legacy of the World War reshaped Europe. Certainly both Elias and Malachy learned to value art and to appreciate those things that made for human development.

The beauty of Rome and its vitality constantly fascinated Elias and he was left with enduring memories of life at so many levels in the Rome of the 1920s.

The Piazza d'Espagna lies at the foot of the Pincio, one of the Seven Hills of Rome. One street as straight as an arrow leads to the Piazza del Populo. It is called the Via del Babuino. A parallel street is called the Via Margutta. The backyards of the shops and houses of the Via del Babuino almost screwed themselves into the rising slopes of the Pincio and if, my dear Cahal, you ever have any doubts about the Seven Hills of Rome spend a few years as a Roman student and you will find that in that apparently flat plain you are always climbing up or climbing down. It was not difficult for me because I am a mountainy man and the calves of my legs were well developed and I like hills. I like the going up and the coming down.

I had a curious mind. I didn't like the crocodile marches out of college and home again, climbing up to the Pincio or up to the Gainiculum. Going down the Via del Babuino we could see in front of us Monti Mario, another of those Seven Hills, but since our hours for footslogging were limited I do not think that we ever climbed Monti Mario. I have heard some American sect bought a site on top of Monti Mario on which they hoped to build something that would rival Saint Peter's, but the Planning Authorities of Rome wisely decided that such a counter attraction would never have the same tourist pull as Saint Peter's and the Vatican.

The quarter that I speak about enclosed by the Via del Babuino and the Via Margutta is the centre of the artistic life of Rome. The people who reside there are a variegated crowd – artists, painters, sculptors, smithies in wrought iron – in fact they embraced every variety of art in its changing fashion. You can walk down the streets window-shopping, as it were, and see a lamp standard, just the very thing your wife wanted, or some other little gadget in wrought iron or brass. Italians are experts in that work. You could listen, as I have, outside the door of a smithy and hear the hammers tinkling on anvils and you knew that a garden gate or an electric light standard, or some other example of wrought iron, was taking shape. Every craftsman likes someone who is interested in his craft and after a while those smithies began to know me, but they regarded me as just being a curious observer. They didn't mind if I walked in and looked at a young fellow, hammering out some design upon the horn of an anvil. What a district that is! Honest smithies, painters, trying to judge the wind of fashion, free livers, most of them living with their mistresses having no interest at all in such curiosities as a friar in brown. To them he was just as interesting as a country mule, and just as ordinary.

Speaking about mules, the district was dotted with wine shops and there was a weekly delivery of wine from the Alban Hills. Every wine-cart had its barrels, sometimes two, sometimes four, drawn by one mule or two as necessity demanded. The driver always had an awning which he could pull down over his head in the noon-day sun and there was always a watchdog; a fierce little terrier type, and no one could approach that cart except over his dead body. You can see these mule wine-carts standing outside a wine shop and the wine is of every variety. Excellent, or just good, or bad, according to your pocket.

Always, of course there was the Italian "pasta". In that district you didn't have to walk fifty yards and be short of a heaped-up plate of macaroni or spaghetti in the Milan, Bologna or Neapolitan style. Wine was the drink, and coffee to cure the headache. That district was full of human variety. Tradesmen, shop-keepers, sculptors, painters, pimps, street women – the lot. Few people paid any attention to the morals or activities of the people next door. Few landladies bothered about the lives of those who lived upstairs; they had enough hardship to scratch a living from the improvident types who lived on the passing mood.

Letters to Cahal, 50.

Elias found himself involved with one particular artist and the resulting tussle says something about the friar's resolution and his judgement.

I knew one man fairly well. He was an artist and he had a big front room which he hired out for one-man shows. One day it would be filled with pictures, another day with ceramics, another with glass, and then again with sculpture of one kind or another. There was one sculptor who had a private income. He spent his whole life upon a masterpiece. It was twenty-feet high and a terrifying spectacle, but day after day he chipped and chipped and stood back and looked and chipped again with rough chisel and fine chisel. I don't know what happened to it in the end, but he used to say it was going to Brazil. Maybe it has ended up in the new capital city of Brasilia – I hope he got paid for it. It became so famous in the end that people used to drop in to see how it was going on. He would work away without even looking at them. If you spoke to him he waved you away as much as to say, 'don't interrupt the profundity of my thought.'

I liked talking to this artist who hired out his front room. The hallway was covered with paintings, mostly small in size. One day I thought that I would seek his advice on a small commission. I had been home to Ireland and during my absence a venerable uncle had passed away and I called to see the family. This man was a noted character but the only trace of him that remained was an old faded photograph showing three quarters of his face. His wife deplored that there was nothing better by which he could be remembered and she asked me if I could do anything to persuade a photographer to make a better reproduction; but I didn't think that was the solution. I decided that I would bring the photo to Rome with me and get some artist to reproduce it in black and white on a sort of biscuit-brown paper to warm it up. I was not trying to reproduce a Leonardo da Vinci cartoon.

I had this faded photo in my pocket one day as I wandered down the street so I let my friend see it. "It's the only surviving photograph of him," I said. He looked at it gravely for a while then said, "Ah, what character! What strength! What a magnificent head! What a pity! If he had lived in the days of Michelangelo he would have become immortal on the roof of the Sistine Chapel." "Perhaps you know some young artist," said I, "who could do a charcoal drawing on a biscuit-coloured paper, with just enough detail to show the sort of man he was?"

My venerable uncle had a face like the Rock of Cashel, a fact not always appreciated by his immediate relations because he was just about as flexible as granite, and he had a sense of humour and a gift of expression equalled by few. "Yes," the man from the gallery said, "I will see what can be done." The fee promised was 5,000 lire.

I left him to it for a month. Then I called in just to see how it was getting on, and he gravely unrolled for me a canvas, in colour, sixteen inches by twenty. This was not what I had wanted and I told him so. "But," said he, "it is disgraceful that your venerable relation should have no other memory than a few lines of charcoal on tinted paper." Was I not proud of him? Had I no respect for the dead? Surely my better feelings should prevail in a matter of this kind. It didn't matter to him, he was not making any money out of it. This he said, and a lot more. I had been looking at

51

the painting waiting patiently for the rain to stop, because the words fell away from him like a torrent from the skies. Then I noticed something about the canvas. I could see the brush marks of shoulders; I could see his collar and tie had been painted in style, but the face looked peculiarly flat. I tilted it to the light and although I could see the varnish on the features I immediately saw what had happened. Some young fellow handy with crayons had drawn the head; someone else had drawn the shoulders; the whole had been sprayed over with a clear varnish to match it up. The man from the gallery saw the look in my eye. He saw the way I tilted the canvas to catch the light and I said to him, "This isn't a painting, it is only half a painting. The features have been done in crayon and the whole sprayed over with varnish." He looked. He took the canvas and tilted it just as I had done and then he turned with a look of blank astonishment on his face. He was speechless. Maybe he had no words for this occasion. He made as if he would tear the thing in two, but compromised by throwing it on the floor. He called upon the Madonna to bear witness how grievously his honour had been compromised by skulduggery. He laid a consoling hand upon my shoulder and promised that in just one week I would have what had been promised me.

I went some time latter with the 5,000 lire and received a very satisfactory drawing of my deceased uncle. The man from the gallery left me for a few moments to get something in which to roll the drawing and then I spied my respected uncle hanging in a quiet corner. By this time the canvas had been spread on a wooden frame and the price was marked 10,000 lire. It now adorns some home in the Middle West of America. I am quite sure the old man, if he still can see the world around him, enjoys the view from the endless prairies.

Letters to Cahal, 51.

On 29th June 1925 Elias and his younger brother Malachy were ordained by Cardinal Pompeii at the Church of Santa Maria in Traspontina. The church where they were ordained today stands on the Via della Conciliazione, the great sweep of road that leads to Saint Peter's. In 1925 the Church which was part of a Carmelite priory was in a maze of streets called the Borgo. It was an area associated in the Middle Ages with English pilgrims. Much of the district was cleared by Mussolini around 1930 and as a result the Church is one of the few old buildings as you approach Saint Peter's.

The Carmelite Church of Santa Maria in Traspontina, Rome.

53

The Carmelite Church of Santa Maria in Traspontina, Rome, with St. Peter's Basilica in the background.

Malachy had joined the Carmelites a short while after his brother, but as he spent only one year at university in Ireland he caught up with Elias whose years as a student had been a longer road. As the two young friars returned to Ireland they left their younger brother Kilian in Rome. Kilian was ordained in 1928 and stayed on to gain his doctorate. Kilian was then sent to work in the United States and the brothers were destined to be separated for more than twenty years. Elias speaks about leaving Rome with a sense of nostalgia and foreboding.

One day after eight years in Roman colleges, I finally packed my bags and faced the road out of Rome. I said to myself "here begins the long haul" … but I have never ceased to be grateful for the protective scaffolding given me by the Carmelite Rule. Now I have come thru' over 45 years of religious life and I still wonder how I escaped the perils of the world.

The Lynch brothers (l-r): Malachy, Elias, Kilian.

Elias believed that Mary, Our Lady, had been a source of protection helping him through the wastelands and desert places of life. However, he had compassionate words for those who were not able to persevere. Elias's reflections were written in 1963 at a time when illness was causing him to reassess his life. At the same time his reflections ring with humour as he remembers his sister Mary teasing him about his choice of life. She reminded him,

55

"God did you a favour when he never allowed you to marry, because there would have been either murder, suicide or manslaughter in the family." I completely agree with her but I can tell you also I have met many women in the course of my life who have told me I am a dead loss. I had only one reply to them all, that once upon a time I nailed my colours to the mast; I never have and never will haul them down.

July Newsletter 1963.

All down the years Elias had a sense of purpose and also a sense of limitation. He grew in his love for the Order and was aware of its strengths and its shortcomings. He was to say, "Certain it is that I could never live in any other kind of religious order. We belong to the least regimented of all the orders in the Church." These comments come from a series of letters he wrote to a fellow Carmelite, Cahal Gallagher. Cahal was a Dubliner, son of a policeman, born in Dublin a few years after Elias. He was a warm-hearted but rumbusteous friar, a man that Elias felt at home with. The letters were a literary device, but Cahal in the writer's mind was more the nodding partner in a conversation. The letters were written in the period from 1961 to 1963 and at times they echo the newsletters Elias wrote over a span of 30 years. Some thoughts from a letter written in 1961 describe something of the motivation that inspired the ministry that Elias was to begin in 1926 on his return from Rome.

My dear Cahal,

I have often heard you say that you could not, or would not, have ever been anything else but a Carmelite. I have said so myself. It is a gross exaggeration because we would neither of us have been Carmelites except by the Will of God. Call it accident or design, but here we are forty years' service in the ranks. We have never amounted to very much, minor command in an unimportant set-up. Mind you, I am not saying that it hasn't been very nice; I am not saying that we have not enjoyed it. You have I know, and you are a better mixer than I am. It took me a long time to find out

56

that ordinary people regarded me as rough and tough, and many of them never had the time to find out that there was, and is, a kinder side to my nature. How many times have you stood before the world, solid on your two feet, trying to look as unshakable as the Rock of Gibraltar, and how many times have you gone back to your room feeling just like a frightened fool.

Letter to Cahal, July 31st 1961.

The Ireland that Elias returned to was just emerging from almost a decade of conflict. The struggle for Irish independence ended with the Treaty that established the Irish Free State, but with the six Northern Counties under British rule. The Civil War that erupted in the period after the Treaty was to leave divisions that would linger on for generations. Among the Carmelites some were ardent Republicans, especially Elias Maggenis who was the Prior General. Others were willing to accept the Treaty while Brocard Taylor – then Prior of Terenure – was very much a 'West Briton' never losing a nostalgia for the monarchy.

Brocard Taylor (front left) with fellow Carmelite scholars.

57

Malachy Lynch celebrating Mass in the ruins of Faversham's medieval Abbey in 1929, the centenary of Catholic Emancipation.

Whitefriars Street on the edge of the city and close to the poorest part of Dublin was a challenging situation for a newly ordained friar. The community cared for a busy church, a number of hospitals, schools and a constant stream of people seeking help because of the reputation of the community. Elias settled into the work with energy but Malachy was sent to England as the Archbishop of Southwark had given the Carmelites two parishes in Kent; Faversham and Sittingbourne. 1926 was to mark the re-founding of the Carmelite Friars in Britain. The new foundation had enthusiastic support but it was a venture of faith as the Irish Carmelites were stretched with commitments in America and Australia. The new foundations in Kent needed financial support and given the economic climate of the time in the aftermath of upheaval in Ireland money was in short supply.

In 1929 Malachy was recalled to Ireland to be Novice Master; he was to hold that post with distinction until he came to Wales in 1936. At the same time Elias was made Prior of the formation community at Ardavon where young friars lived whilst studying at the University or the Jesuit Theology Faculty at

58

Milltown. I remember shortly before his death in 1992 Father Patrick Geary spoke of his time as a student friar and of the impact Elias made on the community. Patrick Geary was to work closely with Elias in later years when he became the first Provincial Superior of the Order in Britain. Pat (as he was known) joined the Order with Cahal Gallagher in 1921; they were barely seventeen at the time.

While Cahal often saw the past in a golden haze, Pat was more forthright in speaking of the hardships and inequalities that were the lot of young friars. A tight demanding timetable was accompanied by meagre food which made life hard for young men who were barely out of their teens. What made matters worse was the knowledge that their seniors fared so much better. It was a mentality that reflected not so much Gospel values but rather that of 'upstairs-downstairs'. As late as the 1960s a Provincial Superior in Ireland was able to say in all seriousness, "Don't you see the priests are like 'officers' and the students are 'the other ranks'." A succinct summary, but far from the spirit of the Carmelite *Rule of Saint Albert*. However, while not excusing such inequalities one only has to think of how junior doctors and many others have been treated.

The young Brother Anthony McGreal (left) with fellow friar Brother Leo, circa 1930.

59

Elias – from his own experience in the Order and his family life – brought humanity to the community at Ardavon. He recognised that if the young friars were to study and live the call of community life they needed decent food and a regime that had a sense of human warmth and understanding, so for a few years life was somewhat more humane at Ardavon. Years later he was to remember the students he cared for, among whom was a future Provincial of the Order in Ireland and Bishop Donal Lamont who was to play a significant role in the life of the Church in Zimbabwe. It was around this time that Elias encouraged a young man from Mayo to join the Order despite his severe hearing impairment. The young man, Anthony McGreal, was to become a friend and loyal co-worker with Elias for some thirty years.

A portrait of Anthony McGreal at Faversham.

60

Anthony McGreal leads the procession of friars returning to Aylesford Priory.

In 1931 the Chapter of the Irish Carmelites asked Elias to go to Sittingbourne in Kent to take over from John Cogan who had pioneered the mission. What began with hope and enthusiasm was to end in near tears, but paradoxically was also to prove a creative moment. Sittingbourne sat astride the A2 road about halfway between London and Dover, about ten miles east of Faversham. The Catholic community was growing and the church just to the east of the town centre was near a convent with a flourishing school, and next to the church was a decent house for the friars. Elias brought with him some years of experience and a desire to serve the people, especially the sick, and to build community. While the majority of the parishioners lived in the town the parish boundaries reached out into the countryside embracing a number of Kentish villages. Sick calls needed transport and we hear of Elias fitting himself into a tiny vehicle to go on his rounds. In one of his letters to Cahal he describes a sick call on a cold winter's night. The atmosphere he evokes is almost Dickensian and his reactions show how reflective and self-conscious

61

he could be. What does come out is a great sense of honesty, and at the ending of the story his obvious respect for the Salvation Army is an example of ecumenism at a time when Christians tended to remain separate.

One cold winter's night I didn't like the howl of the wind and I retired to bed early. It was a really cold December. I was nicely settled in bed when the door bell rang. I waited a while and finally went down in my dressing gown to find a woman on the step. "Come in". The wind was driving the sleet like a knife through the privet hedge before the door. I knew she was from Lancashire by her accent. "Father, we have been having a week down in Milton Regis and there is an old Catholic woman living there and I think she is dying." I took the name and the address. She told me how to find the house and I said I would see about it early in the morning. I went back to my bed and tried to make up my mind. It was a losing battle! I dressed and found the necessary elements for a sick call and faced the night.

Between the presbytery and Milton Regis there is a maze of dark, dismal streets housing the workers of an old paper mill that was still in production. I found my way to Milton Regis with the skirts of my habit around my head. I remember rolling my scapular up and tucking it inside my cincture while I sorted out with at torch the door numbers of that miserable street. I found the place. The door was open. I went upstairs and knocked at the door. There was no answer so I opened it and went in. A gaslight was hanging from the ceiling. I tried to light it, but there was no gas in the pipes. Then I saw a shilling slot meter in the corner and I was lucky to have a shilling. I turned on the light, and lit the gas fire, and turned round to look for the sick woman. The bed was pushed against the wall and she was lying on the far side. Her husband was on the outside and I had to bend over him to make sure she was the woman I wanted to see. I tried to get him out of bed to sit in the chair before the fire, but all I got from him was a very negative grunt. He wasn't going anywhere. I saw that I would have to carry on without his help.

The poor old woman was lying partly on her side, whimpering like a wounded animal; it was the most awful sound I have ever

62

heard. I explained who I was, that I had come to give her the Last Sacraments. I explained what they were and that it would not take long. There was no obligation to confess in the hearing of another, so I said the introductory prayers and asked her to think of the good God and of anything she had done wrong in her life and for which she was sorry. I told her that our religious obligations concerned first our duties to God himself, our duty to our neighbour, and finally our duty to ourselves. She stopped whimpering and I said to her, "Now think, and hold my hand while you do it." After a little while I said, "I am going to give you absolution", then I gave her Holy Viaticum bending over the old man at her side. Then I explained that Extreme Unction could only be given in a short form merely by anointing the forehead, that the Sacrament was valid in that form and that sometimes it brought considerable relief both of mind and body to those who were ill. I anointed her in the short form, and turned to wipe my fingers on the cotton wool and to screw the cap back on the capsule of oil. I had put the sick call set on a chair near the bottom of the bed. As I stood with my back to the old man I felt something rubbing against the calf of my leg. I turned to find that he was pushing me with his toe. He had his sock on, and at first I thought he was giving me a little encouragement to go home. I turned round to him and said, "It's nearly all over now." "Wot abaut me?" he said. "Are you Catholic too?" said I. I got no answer except, "Maybe". That put me on the spot. I didn't know whether he was a Catholic or not. Perhaps he was only jealous and wanted as much done for him as for his wife. I asked a few more questions and all I got from him was, "I am sick too." I finally decided that he had asked me for the Last Sacraments and I went through the same routine with him, conditional absolution, Extreme Unction, but I didn't give him Holy Viaticum. I was in great doubt about the whole thing, but I found him holding my left hand as if he didn't want to let go. In the end I gave them both the general absolution and the last blessing, which is the Papal blessing. I held their hands and said a few ejaculations for them and took the holding of the hands as their agreement. Then I left for home. I was resolved to be back in the morning and try to make some amends for what I looked upon as a very patchy job.

63

As I went home through those black dirty streets there was a policeman standing at the crossroads. It was near two o'clock in the morning. He stepped out into the road as if to intercept me and I stopped. I saw him looking at the little case I carried under my arm. I could see the puzzlement in his face and I said, "I have been down to Milton Regis on a sick call to an old woman who is dying." "Funny crowd, those Miltonians," he said, "you don't know whether you are coming or going with them." "I did," said I, "I have a definite impression I was going." He said, "They don't call you out at this time of night, do they?" "Oh yes," I said, "we belong to the fire brigade and we are always on call." He walked with me to the main London Road; the Presbytery was just across the street. I had the impression he wanted to see where I was going and my humour was distinctly cold towards the policeman. I said to him, "Did you ever hear of the fiddler of Dooney?" "I can't say I have," he said, "Why?" "Well, if you had heard of the fiddler of Dooney you would be able to tell me what I am thinking about now. Good night!"

Have you ever mentally walloped yourself all the way home from doing something because you are not pleased with the way you had done it? That night I did; and I did all through a sleepless night. I said to myself, "You are a priest. You are called to administer the Sacraments. You are bound to ensure the proper conditions under which they can be given to men. What has happened to your theology? Did you ever learn any, or is it just that you have forgotten it? How did you know she was a Catholic or that he was a Catholic, and yet you flung the Sacraments at them just as if they were practising Catholics? You never saw either of them in your life. You are under a grave obligation to preserve the validity of the Sacraments and not to throw them around as if you owned them. Sacraments were instituted by Christ as a means of grace to human souls. How did you know that these people were even married to each other? How did you know that they were ever baptised? There are dozens of ways in which a priest can be a fool, but you seem to have covered most of them." I went back next morning. To my surprise the old woman was sitting in a chair beside the window. She had a coat over her night gown. She looked very cold and miserable and gave a little whimper now and then, but she looked at me with a degree of welcome. There was a screen around the bed. I looked towards it and said to her, "How is your husband?" She said, "He is dead." There was a finality about the way she said it that almost told the end of time. I said, "Have you had any breakfast?" She shook her head. I went down to a café on the main street; I told the woman how things were and inside a few minutes she had a tray of tea and some scones ready. I offered to pay for them and she refused. I offered to carry them for her and she would not let me. She carried the tray around the corner and up the stairs and I sat by while she poured scalding tea for the old woman. She drank four cups of tea before she touched a scone, then she munched slowly and silently. I decided I would find a policeman and I was right lucky. As I crossed the main street a police car came from the direction of Sheerness and it was a Police Inspector, his driver and two other people in the back. I stopped the car and he said, "Hang on for a while and I will send the sergeant back to see you." I waited until the sergeant came back in the car and from there on the matter was out of my hands. The old lady moved to the infirmary; she died there two days later and I buried the two of them.

I still had not cleared my mind as to whether I had done right or wrong.

Some days later I met the woman who had started me out on that black night. She was a Salvation Army Lieutenant doing relief work for a few weeks in Sittingbourne. The Salvation Army Citadel was nearly opposite our church and one evening I popped in. She was having a choir practice. I thanked her for what she had done. I told her that she had done a work of Good – one of the corporal works of mercy and that God would surely reward her. She was indeed grateful and so were the Salvation lassies gathered around her. "How did you know that the woman was a Catholic, because I couldn't get a word out of her?" She said, "I couldn't get a word out of her either; all I could hear was 'Jesus, Mary and Joseph', and I know that it is a Lancashire prayer used by Catholics." Then I knew that I had done right and that God had guided me, aided by the Salvation Army girl.

Father Cogan, who had preceded me in Sittingbourne, used to stand outside the church on Sunday morning to greet the people as

65

they came to the eleven o'clock Mass. The Salvation Army used to lead a parade down the main street to where they held their prayer meeting at the other end of town. They never interfered with us because they marched by at ten to eleven before Mass began. But thereafter I used to stand upon the step and salute their flag as it went by. Not merely did they stop playing as they passed the church, but went past with a pleasant smile. I distinctly remember, for the remaining months I stayed in Sittingbourne, meeting old ladies on the street who smiled at me with real affection and gave me a modest bow.

Letter to Cahal, 3rd Oct 1962. A Sick Call.

It was Elias's urge to build community, to create a social dimension to the parish, that was to bring his stay at Sittingbourne to an abrupt end. Elias opened a social club with a bar to draw parishioners together and with a hope of helping parish funds. However, events beyond Elias's control spelt disaster for the venture. What was more the *News of the World* tabloid caught scent of the story with Elias appearing as 'mine host of the Whitefriars Arms' giving the impression that he was running a sleazy pub. The Archbishop was not amused, while back in Ireland things were in turmoil after a bewildering visitation of the Province by Brocard Taylor who had decided that all was not well with the Carmelites. In the context of Brocard's fulminations Elias's problems were cast in the context of what was regarded as an overall state of chaos. Reflecting on events years later Elias said:

That was enough to wreck a very large battleship let alone a very small schooner like me. When the solemn conclave of the Carmelite elders met in Dublin they shook their heads and considered what should be done. It was near the time of the Provincial Chapter and I was sent into exile in Faversham where I couldn't possibly do any more harm. They were right! It took me two years to recover my equilibrium and another Chapter passed into history.

A New Parish Priest

Rev M. E. Lynch, O.Chrm.,
D.Phr D.D., of Ballymanus House,
Aughrin, Co. Wicklow, who has been
appointed Parish Priest of Faversham,
Kent.—Lafayette.

A brief announcement of Faversham's new priest in a newspaper.

The Chapter meeting in Dublin in 1934 appointed Elias to Faversham but left his brother Malachy as Novice Master in Kinsale. One interesting appointment was the naming of Kilian Lynch as Prior of Kinsale. Kilian had gone to the United States after gaining his Masters Degree and Doctorate in Rome and was teaching philosophy. It would seem that the powers-that-be wanted him back in Ireland where his gifts could be put to good use. However, Kilian viewed the change with some trepidation and persuaded the Provincial to allow him to stay on in America. Within a short time he became Prior Provincial of the newly-formed New York Province, and in 1947 he became Prior General of the Order. Meanwhile, Elias was not to realise that his life was to be given its definitive direction as he was to remain in Faversham until his death thirty-three years later in 1967. "I was left where I was."

Elias felt his move to Faversham was some sort of punishment, yet the Provincial John Cogan was committed to the venture in Kent and was by no means hard-hearted. Perhaps in his eyes Elias was being given a challenge and he believed that Elias had the energy and resourcefulness to do something creative in Faversham. John Cogan knew the place, the problems, and perhaps hoped that despite the seeming debacle in Sittingbourne Elias would have

67

the energy and insight to make a go of Faversham. It is true the Catholic population was sparse and there were few financial resources. East Kent in those days was decidedly rural and was, if anything, still able to harbour a less than positive view of Catholicism. Catholics were few and mainly foreign.

Elias left a vivid description of his arrival in Faversham.

> I well remember the first day I walked up *Stone Street*. I saw twin towers opposite the chapel, and for a moment I was deluded. I said to myself, "This cannot be true!" They were the twin towers of the Anglican chapel in the Almshouses, and when I read the notice board outside I knew I was off my beam. I asked a passer-by, "Where is the Catholic Church around here?" He said to me, "You will find it just up there behind a wall." I went in search of it. I found a little place like a minor garage, a garden and a big rambling house, and little else. There was no bath, and little furniture, but to make up for this there were four different ground entrances to the place. Downstairs you never knew when someone would rap upon the French windows and demand to be let in. A previous occupant had left two club chairs, one of which I claimed as my own, and in that ground-floor room we had a coal fire and there I warmed my feet.
>
> My first Sunday in the Faversham Mission yielded 17/6d. in the collection – two Masses, catechism and evening devotions – at a time when the Provincial of the Irish Province couldn't afford to give me anything better than half a crown Mass stipends. We had to pay rates, insurance, electricity and coal. I had a lay-brother to look after me. He was a devoted character, but no cook. A few devoted women helped out; we had hot steak and kidney pie on Sundays which lasted until Wednesday and Brother Franco cooked enough vegetables to last until then. Frankly, I do not know how I came through. I walked around the town and came to the conclusion that the place would never allow me to buy more than shoe leather. I determined I would stay in Faversham only six months, and no longer. I have now been here thirty-one years.

68

What is the explanation of that? I had made up my mind. I said, "If these people have not the heart to support me, if they do not give me enough to feed me, I will become a beggar." That is how I first began to use the post.

Carmelite News February-April 1962.
The Trials of a Missionary.

Elias became a beggar and in doing so lived out his Carmelite calling; working in order to live and relying on the Providence of God. However, he was still in the prime of his life, still in his thirties full of ideas and resilience. The parishioners found his vigour disconcerting and certainly they were unused to his direct and forthright way of dealing with things. Elias was convinced they thought he was mad.

In 1935 Anthony McGreal joined him at Faversham. Anthony had been allowed to become a friar despite his hearing disability and was to be a loyal and hard-working collaborator.

Elias realised that he needed to reach a wider constituency than the parish if he was to finance his apostolate and so a newsletter began promoting devotion to Saint Thérèse of Lisieux, the Infant Jesus and Saint Jude the Apostle. A mailing list was gradually built up and soon the first goal was achieved of finding a new site for the church and priory. The church in Plantation Road reminded Elias of a garage and the house in his eyes was a disaster. By the middle of 1935 Elias was negotiating with Stidolph's, a Faversham estate agent, to buy the old Bible School and teachers' house in Tanners Street, quite close to the almshouses that he admired. The Bible School had been built in 1861 but in 1910 had become the Empire Picture Hall. A new cinema had been built in the centre of Faversham so the old school became vacant as did the adjacent house which had served as accommodation for the Bible School's teachers. Elias was able to buy the buildings and by 1937 the Carmelites were established in Tanners Street. The house was a fine Georgian building dating

Drawing by a sister from Sittingbourne of the exterior of the Church of Our Lady of Mount Carmel in Tanners Street.

from 1743, the home of John Gilbert, a tanner, and the property came with an extensive garden. The cost of the whole complex was £900.

Elias described the old school building as a sorry wreck of a place but with the help of craftsmen and artists the site came alive. The murals in the sanctuary by Edward Ardizzone are now recognised as masterpieces. Elias, like his brother Malachy, had a love of art and neither would have any truck with what passed for church art at that time. The old church and house in Plantation Road were to become a convent from which the Notre Dame Sisters conducted a Primary School.

The move to Tanners Street gave scope for a more satisfactory site for the Priory and the large garden was to enable further development that would include an office and a print shop. It was about this time that Elias began to get involved

70

*Interior of the Church of Our Lady of Mount Carmel at Faversham,
with murals in the sanctuary by Edward Ardizzone.*

in the life of the town. He became a town councillor and served on the council for some fourteen years. These years would include the Second World War and the difficult years that followed wartime. Elias was to be Chairman of the Housing, Town Planning and Industrial Development committees. Beside that role he was involved at county level advising on planning and education. His lasting memorial in Faversham is his achievement of ensuring that a decent stock of council houses were built after the war. In his view politics was a way of serving the people, an integral part of ministry. He therefore always stood as an independent with the slogan "Don't flinch – vote for Lynch." This involvement with local affairs enabled him to become part of the social life of the town making many friendships that would give him practical support for the Order and the Church at large. Among these friends were Harry Knowles, Harry Oldfield and many others including Prince Andrew Romanov, a cousin of Czar Nicholas who lived at Provender just outside Faversham.

71

If anything Elias had the energy and stamina of a countryman and so the wide variety of tasks that he took on did not overwhelm him but were to take their toll later in his life. In 1938 he set up the Carmelite Press so that he could produce the newsletter and other literature. At the same time he took on preaching engagements and found sympathetic listeners especially in Lancashire. During the rest of his life he always felt at ease when he heard a Lancashire accent. His contact with the parishes where he talked about Saint Thérèse, Our Lady and the Carmelite scapular added numbers to the newsletter mailing list back at Faversham. Brother Anthony and a band of helpers ensured that names were recorded and envelopes addressed.

The war years were a time of difficulty and danger. Faversham was not far from the Channel coast and in the late summer of 1940 the Battle of Britain raged in the skies of Kent. Then came the waves of bombers heading for London, the Blitz that carried on into 1941 and then the V-bombs. While Faversham was never a target as such, enough stray bombs fell to cause fear and havoc. It was a time of rationing, of austerity, and with petrol-rationing and blackout travel was restricted. The difficulties did not daunt Elias, and his work in Faversham was to increase if anything. The wartime saw a growth in the Little Flower Society and devotion to Saint Jude was to grow beyond

Prior Is New Mayor Of Kentish Town

VERY Rev. Father Elias Lynch, O.Carm., Prior, Faversham, Kent, who has been elected Mayor of the town, is a native of Aughrim, Co. Wicklow, and one of a family of 13, 11 of whom are living.

He is a brother of Very Rev. Dr. Killian Lynch, O.Carm., Prior-General of the Order in Rome; Very Rev. Father Malachi Lynch, O.Carm., Prior, Aylesford, Kent; and Rev. Mother Mary Andrew, of the Sisters of Mercy in Australia. He is also a brother of Mr. James Lynch, Portobello, and Mr. Thomas Lynch, Rathmines, Dublin. Their home was Ballymanus House, Aughrim, which was the ancient home of the O'Byrnes of Wicklow, of whom the celebrated Billy O'Byrne, one of the leaders of the 1798 Rising, was one.

Very Rev. Father Elias, who has been a member of the Faversham

Very Rev. Father Lynch

Council for 14 years, was Chairman of the Housing Committee and responsible for a number of housing schemes. He was educated at Terenure College, Dublin, and joined the Order there and then went to Rome to complete his studies in the Carmelite College, where he was ordained in 1927. He returned to Ireland and served in Whitefriar St. for some years and then became Prior of Ardavon, Orwell Rd., Rathgar.

An Irish newspaper feature prematurely reported on a hope dashed.

expectation. In that time of danger people felt drawn to the Apostle who gave hope where otherwise fear could have prevailed. Both Elias and Brother Anthony were amazed at the demand for prayer cards, and despite paper-rationing hundreds of thousands of pictures of Saint Jude were distributed. Paper-rationing meant that the *Carmelite News* appeared on roughly recycled paper and much reduced in size, but it did appear.

Shortage of food was also part of life in those days and Elias thanked those who sent butter and the occasional pound of rashers. However he was conscious of

> ... the thousands of refugees, homeless and persecuted on the roads of Europe, bombed and machine gunned and starved, of mothers dying with their children in their arms, seeing them, perhaps left homeless and deserted by the last light of their eyes. What has life meant to them but to lose it all? I often think that these are the people who die and remain forever uncanonised. But God has given them this vision of the Kingdom: 'God shall wipe away all tears from their eyes and death shall be no more'.
>
> *Carmelite News* November 1944.

In 1942 Elias produced a *Soldier's Prayer*; a profession of faith in times of danger which he printed on the back of a small card bearing the picture of Our Lady of Mount Carmel.

I believe in one God. I believe that God rewards the good, and punishes the wicked.

I believe that in God there are three Divine Persons – God the Father, God the Son, and God the Holy Ghost.

I believe that God the Son became man, without ceasing to be God. I believe that He is my Lord and my Saviour, the Redeemer of the human race, that He died on the Cross for the salvation of all men, that He died also for me.

I believe, on God's authority, everything that He has taught and revealed.

O MY GOD, give me strong faith. O my God, help me to believe with lively faith.

O MY GOD, Who art all-good and all-merciful, I sincerely hope to be saved. Help me to do all that is necessary for my salvation.

I have committed many sins in my life, but now I turn away from them, and hate them, I am sorry, truly sorry for all of them, because I have offended Thee, who art all-good, all-perfect, all-holy, all-merciful and kind, and Who died on the Cross for me.

I LOVE Thee, O my God, with all my heart. Please forgive me for having offended Thee.

I promise, O God, that with Thy help, I will never offend Thee again.

MY GOD, HAVE MERCY ON ME.

There was a lighter side in the war years. Elias ends a newsletter in 1941 with the following words:

God bless and protect you all! Say a prayer for us that we may be spared the dangers that surround us. We have a good Air Raid Shelter but we cannot stay in it all the time.

In the same newsletter Elias comments,

> We have even got Adolf Hitler as a member of the Little Flower Society, although he does not know about it. A good Protestant lady wrote to ask us what was to be done about Adolf Hitler. We suggested he became a member of the Little Flower Society and maybe our prayers would either kill or cure him. Up to the present we have not noticed any particular change in his health.
>
> *Carmelite News* 1942.

Quite a few soldiers were stationed in the Faversham area and some of their nocturnal activities impinged on the Carmelite community. Elias recounts a very human incident and his handling of the matter shows his humanity which is in the end rewarded!

> They say that conscience goes to sleep during war because values change so rapidly.
>
> In Tanners Street we live beside the church and the house is a little bit back from the street and there is a little forecourt in front of the house with an outer door.
>
> Opposite us in the closing years of the war lived a blonde matron with her equally blonde daughter. It is the end cottage in a row built in the 1870s. A little alley way runs beside this end cottage and the lady and her daughter used to entertain the troops. They were both well used to providing sedatives. Every night there would be a collection of soldiers up the little alley way and standing around outside. Such houses were well known to the military authorities and were officially placed out of bounds. That was not intended to warn visitors away, but rather to warn them that peace and good order must be observed on all occasions otherwise they would find themselves on a court martial for breach of the peace and for being out of bounds. The squad cars that toured the area when the pubs shut knew the value of courtesy and co-operation so as they came

75

round the elbow of the street they gave three loud blasts on the horn and that was the signal for the waiting men to slip up the alley. Unfortunately they discovered that it was much easier to slip into the forecourt of our house and there they would hang over the low wall looking down the garden, quietly smoking a cigarette and talking in whispers. My room was directly overhead and in through the open windows on balmy evenings floated that desultory kind of conversation common among men who are out on a spree. After a while I got tired of it, although I didn't lose my interest. I began to think that maybe I could be accused of silent co-operation or tacit agreement.

One afternoon I went to have a talk with the good lady. It was a pleasant conversation; I told her I had no wish to interfere in her private affairs but some of her friends who called around late at night were invading our forecourt so as not to be seen by the squad car and would she ask them to leave us in peace. "Oh, Father," she said, "they are very well-behaved indeed, I never let anybody come near the place under the rank of sergeant." "Well," said I, "I am glad you know where to draw the line. I would not like to see them losing their stripes without cause." She asked me if I felt better because she had heard that I was not very well and we parted good humouredly enough. I came back to sit in my chair beside the window and wondered to myself if I had been too tolerant, but then I reflected that these were lonely men, here today and that maybe in a tomorrow not far distant they would be lying beneath the soil of some Flanders field. I couldn't find it in my heart to do anything else but pray for them. I had little to forgive and in many ways little to endure, so I prayed that a merciful God would look kindly on them and forgive the lapses of their human frailty.

I felt much better after that. Towards the end of the week I was sitting in my chair when I heard the gate to the forecourt being pushed open and when I opened the door there stood Blondie smiling all over her face. She pushed a heavy parcel into my hand and said, "Father, with the compliments of the sergeants' mess." It was a leg o' mutton.

76

I looked at it, and I wondered, and in the end I sent out for a bunch of parsley because I hate roast mutton. It must be boiled and white parsley sauce poured over it before you put a knife in it.

Letter to Cahal, 27.

Perhaps as a result of these events Elias organized a social club for soldiers, providing a few home comforts. The club was in Newton Road and was to close after D-Day. Despite the air raids, the restrictions and the rationing, Elias's work of fundraising continued. However, he was now helping not just the parish in Faversham but the work of his Order in Wales and Ireland.

In 1935 Bishop McGrath of Menevia invited the Carmelites to take over Saint Mary's College and parish in Aberystwyth. Malachy Lynch was chosen to be Prior of the new foundation which involved the pastoral care of a large area of mid-Wales and the running of what was a junior seminary. Malachy, helped in the main by Father Patrick Geary, threw himself into the task. While they did all they could money was needed and soon Elias was helping fund the mission. However, Wales was not the only place to need assistance and soon the call came from Ireland to help the education of the young friars, some of whom would work in England and Wales. Relations with Ireland became less easy when John Cogan was replaced as Provincial by James Carmel O'Shea. John Cogan had served the Order as either Provincial or pioneer for many long years and seemed to have had the gift of holding people together as well as enabling progress to happen. James – or Jimmie – O'Shea was a zealous man, determined and keen to ensure that observance was maintained. While he was a contemporary of Elias their world views would have been diametrically opposed. Jimmie O'Shea would be seen as one who would overturn the notion of the Carmelites as being "the least regimented of all orders."

Upper row: Declan Sugru and Barry Cogan
Lower row: James Carmel O'Shea, J. Stanislaus Megannety, Malachy Lynch.

It is a measure of Elias that over the difficult war years he kept meeting the demands that were made of him. He faced into the wartime situation with energy, and also was inspired by the compassion of Christ and by a personal love of God. Religion was not a case of 'being correct' but of trusting in love. It was this deep-down conviction that enabled Elias to cope with demands and ensure that the money he raised was guarded with careful stewardship. So over the years he was quite ingenious with schemes for raising money, unashamed to be a blatant beggar but also careful to ensure that legal safeguards were in place. Elias ensured that the whole enterprise should have a proper framework so he helped establish a charitable trust to both benefit the Order and to enable transparency. Over the war years he kept those involved carefully informed through a constant flow of correspondence, as often travel and face-to-face meeting was not that easy. Given the fact that the letters were censored I often wonder what the censor made of his letters and the long – often anxious – replies from Dublin. Elias's efforts enabled a new House of Studies to be set up in Dundrum to the South of Dublin, as Ardavon the existing student centre was no longer adequate to house the growing number of students.

At times Elias could be angry, exasperated and blunt. In every organisation – religious orders being no exception – it's all too easy to see legal and financial matters as tedious and not as exciting as the task in hand. Again, it is possible to be disingenuous. Elias had supported his brother's efforts in Wales with patience and loyalty, but Malachy could be vague and ready to ignore what was mundane. In 1945 Elias felt let down by his brother who had seemingly implied that Elias kept him in the dark and was difficult to deal with. Now, while the brothers had deep bonds of love Elias was always forthright, and a letter from April 1945 shows his feelings, frustration and amazement.

Whitefriars, Faversham, Kent.
19th April 1945.

Dear Father Malachy,

I am sending you a document to be signed and witnessed by the three names at the head of the contract. Will you do so and return immediately to Barclays Bank. You must all three initial the deletion – Trustees of Saint Mary's College Building Fund.

It is very dangerous sending up these things to Saint Mary's College because evidently you don't read what comes in the post.

The Provincial came down here in an awful flap saying that you fellows had your hands in the air declaring that you never had any advice about the Interest Fund, that you had no proof or indication that anything like money existed towards a new college. In fact, that you did not know anything at all about anything.

Now, to say the least of it, this is rank dishonesty because I assured you when I came up last that we had at least fifteen thousand pounds (£15,000) but all you people can do when the Provincial comes is to shrug your shoulders and declare that you don't know anything about anything.

79

It doesn't encourage anyone to work for your interests, and I think it may do good to tell you that.

At any rate, I asked the Provincial to tell you (since my word is not good enough) that we have over nineteen thousand pounds (£19,000) in actual securities etc.; that we have fifteen hundred (£1,500) in the bank, which is not yet invested. Moreover, according to the bank records <u>you have been advised every six months</u> of the state of the Interest Fund. Also, years ago, both you and Father Geary were made the beneficiaries of the Fund; you actually drew upon the Fund to the extent of one hundred and one pounds (£101) for repairs to the college on one occasion. Why then, have you got the sauce to say that you know nothing about the Interest Fund?

I asked the Provincial to suggest to you that you invest five hundred pounds (£500) of the Interest in Trustee Securities. If you leave it to the discretion of the bank manager in Faversham he will suggest to you a security. If you like to send me a cheque for £500 on the Interest Fund I can reinvest it with surplus monies I have in hand, but I would prefer you to do it yourselves.

I hope that we will not hear any more of you people not knowing anything about anything. Also, I want to tell you that I am very fed up with you, I've tried to tell you as completely as possible how matters stood and the best you can do in return is to throw doubt upon the whole position.

Well, I hope I make my sentiments quite clear.

Our Lady keep you!

Elias

Whatever the feelings expressed the bonds between the brothers would be strong despite outbursts of annoyance over the years. What Elias was beginning to realise was that the Carmelite communities in Britain needed autonomy if the Order was to grow. Already a number of friars were in the House of Studies in Dublin who had been born in England and the hope was that more might join. The road to establishing autonomy would be first to establish a commissariat with limited self-governance, before erecting a province separate from Ireland. Writing to Malachy in 1946 Elias weighed the pros and cons of such a move and counselled caution; though sometime later when he realised that their younger brother Kilian could be elected Prior General he then signalled some firmer sense of hope.

23rd May 1946.

Dear Malachy,

Thanks for your letter.

The opinion down here is that it is premature to speak of a commissariat. Father Fitzgerald is in favour of it, but Father Bulbert is definitely against it, and Father O'Malley thinks it is premature. Father Scally and Father Berthistle are willing to be persuaded in favour.

We are all agreed that some flexible sort of arrangement should be come into in regard to Wales. That it should have its own students earmarked for the Mission. Something on the same lines as operated in favour of New York and Australia in our early days. You will remember that the New York business was not a much stronger position than Wales or England, and that it hung fire for a long time until their own students were ordained.

If we get flexible arrangements by which we could have, say, fifteen or twenty students for England and Wales going through, then after ordination of the first seven or ten we could talk of a commissariat with some hope of stability. But I think it is premature to speak of it in the present circumstances.

You see, we have not over here anything that corresponds to a really strong foundation. The foundation of any separation must be based on students in actual training earmarked for the Mission, and within appropriate sight of ordination.

We can all see that a commissariat must come in the end, and on this we are all agreed.

Moreover, until the Roman end has been re-organised under a new General, and until the new General has held a visitation and acquainted himself with the circumstances, any presentation of our case would be prejudiced by the Irish Provincial. He, naturally, would have the biggest say, and the Roman Authorities would not

81

have any intimate appreciation of the position. My suggestion is to shelve the problem until the General's visitation and fight the matter out then. Meanwhile, we can sound the Gremiales [members of the Chapter] and the new Definitory [the Provincial Council] upon the possibility of a gentlemen's agreement about students.

Any more news about the Bishopric? I rather think that we have not the influence to pull it off, but it is a big step forward to be mentioned in connection with it.

I am off to Switzerland on May 28th for a fortnight's holiday. I am feeling pretty good at the moment.

Our Lady keep you!

Elias.

It was about this time in 1945 that I first met Elias Lynch. I had come down to Kent with my parents to see Brother Anthony, my uncle, and as the war in Europe was ended travel was possible even though the journey from Manchester to London took seven hours; then the mystery of the Underground and escalators and another train with green Southern Railway carriages. I remember the Sunderland flyboats moored in the Medway at Rochester close by the Castle and Cathedral.

Elias seemed different from other priests I had met, with his Panama hat and light summer jacket sitting in the garden near what then was the office under the church, a hub of activity. Everything was warm and sunny after the blackout of war and the welcome was equally warm.

In the years following the war and before diabetes took hold Elias enjoyed travelling to Lausanne, Paris and the States while the General Chapter of 1947 brought him back to Rome for the first time since 1925. As a man who worked hard he felt he owed himself some care and kindness. He enjoyed life, he was sociable, he appreciated good food and drink, and while deep-down shy and self-conscious he liked women but seemed to feel he would always get

The Provincial Chapter in Dublin 1946. Elias is third from the left on the middle row, and central in the detail below. Fr. Patrick Geary appears in the same row, second on Elias's left.

83

it wrong. The superiors who pulled him down a peg after Sittingbourne were gone; James Carmel O'Shea would have liked to rein him in but in the end Elias's forthrightness was too much. In later years another Provincial superior would arrive in Faversham breathing fire only to find that Elias's personal kindness was utterly disarming. What I always remember was his preference for a decent car with room for a big man. Towards the end of his life when his brother Kilian was Provincial superior he made Elias get rid of the Rover and suggested a Morris Minor. Elias regarded such a vehicle as "a motorised perambulator."

Later in the summer of 1946, at a provincial chapter in Dublin, Elias was appointed a delegate to the General Chapter which was to take place in 1947. While Elias was confirmed in his work in Faversham the role of Prior and Parish Priest was given to Father Edwin Scally, a young priest who had been a novice under Malachy. Elias announced the changes in a dramatic manner in the autumn newsletter of September - October 1946.

I AM STILL HERE

Are you leaving Faversham? NO, I AM NOT LEAVING FAVERSHAM. I remain on as Director of the Carmelite Press and Editor of the "Carmelite News".

For some years I have been feeling the pressure of work and responsibility. Food-rationing has upset my system a little, and I am now on a diet. I have served the local Borough Council for many years. I am Chairman of the Housing and Town Planning and Industrial Development Committee. I am on the North-East Kent Town and Country Planning Committee. It has meant a lot of worry and responsibility. Now that the war is over, I feel that I must concentrate on the really important work that I am called upon to do, and give all my time and attention to the Carmelite Press and to the work of our Societies. Father Scally has become Prior of Whitefriars, and this relieves me of much responsibility for the ordinary routine of the house.

The Provincial Chapter appointed me Delegate to the General Chapter at Rome which is to be held sometime in 1947. Its main business will be to elect the new General of the Order. It will involve my absence from Faversham for about three weeks. It will be nice to visit Rome again after twenty-five years, and it should be a memorable Chapter. While on the one hand the Order has grown in members and prestige in the English-speaking countries, yet we have to deplore the collapse of the Polish and Austrian Provinces. The Dutch Province, which was one of the strongest in the whole Order, has also suffered badly. The Italian and German Provinces are in better state than one could expect. There will be a tremendous amount of reconstruction to be put in hand. I hope to meet in Rome my younger brother, Father Kilian Lynch, who is Provincial in the New York Province. I have not seen him for nearly twenty years. The years run away so quickly, and one hardly realises that those who part in youth can meet again as old men. At any rate, I am still in Faversham, and hope to inflict my propaganda upon you for a few more years.

Carmelite News September-October 1946.

Elias had originally in 1934 been appointed to Faversham when it had been a struggling parish, almost a missionary outpost. Now, twelve years later, the parish was growing but the fundraising and apostolate that had grown alongside it was more than one man could oversee. For the next twenty years Elias was to direct the Press and oversee the Order's finances, and through the newsletter keep in contact with thousands in Britain and Ireland. The money raised helped projects near at home as well as the new missions in Zimbabwe. Much of the energy and money to buy back Aylesford Priory came from nearby Faversham and the Order's apostolate today continues to depend on those who are loyal friends of the Carmelites through the work begun by Elias.

Edwin Scally was an ideal choice to work with Elias, a gentle, prayerful man, loveable and loved by all who knew him. However, over the years confreres

85

came who did not see eye-to-eye with Elias who in turn regarded them as "one-man secret societies" or perhaps seeing the role of Prior as one of power and a stepping-stone to preferment. Elias always had a very wry sense of humour about ambition, aware that the pole of success was greasy and the coming-down could be painful. Food was always important for Elias and it became more of an issue when he became a diabetic. He detested meanness in matters of food; cutting back in the kitchen was false economy and he was to complain of one confrere that he had reduced the community's food to the level of a 1s./9d. canteen.

In the summer of 1947 Elias returned to Rome after an interval of twenty-one years. He was a delegate to the General Chapter. The General Chapter was to elect his youngest brother Kilian as Prior General. It was the first time the brothers had met since their student days in Rome. They made quite a contrast: Kilian tall, austere, academic, with phenomenal stamina and a near-photographic memory; Elias, while equally dynamic, was much more down-to-earth and lacked Kilian's air of austerity. There was much more of the man of affairs about him.

Elias left an account of the Chapter and Papal Audience in the autumn newsletter of 1947. His description of the Papal Audience indicates something of the magnetism and mystique that surrounded Pius XII at that time. Elias saw the Pope as almost from another world and hoped that by his words his readers could make contact with such a figure.

> The last time I wrote, I was about to leave for Rome to attend the General Chapter of the Order. Rome has changed amazingly in 21 years and I hardly knew the place. It must be the noisiest city on earth – no silencers in cars, motor cycles or lorries. The people get really alive at about eleven o'clock at night and then out comes the old concertina. Their voices are pitched about three tones higher than we are used to, so that one gets the impression that they are trying to shout each other down. It is nothing worse

than a leisurely release of spirits after the heat of the sweltering day.

The General Chapter was impressive and interesting. The Cardinal Protector was ill and could not preside, but he sent the Vice Regent of Rome instead. It was a joy to hear the Latin sentences roll off his tongue as he gave the opening address. I found myself wondering if in any language under the sun can human thought and dignity be expressed with such order and grace as the speech of the Ancient Romans.

The business of the Chapter was the election of a new General. The choice fell on the Very Reverend Edward Kilian Lynch, Provincial of the New York Province. As I went forward in my turn to kiss his hand before the Altar as a token of obedience, I kept saying to myself, "Isn't it queer to be going up to kiss the hand of your youngest brother as Prior General of the Order?"

Of course it wasn't queer, because I felt very proud of him, and I felt prouder still of the old Irish Province of the Carmelites that it had now given for a second time a Prior General to the Carmelites.

Fr. Kilian is the youngest of a family of nine brothers and four sisters, and like the rest of us he was born in the Wicklow Mountains near the Vale of Avoca. May God prosper his efforts in the land of Carmel.

When the Chapter was over we were all received in solemn audience by His Holiness. I have seen three Popes – Benedict XV, Pius XI and now Pius XII. When one goes to see the Pope one is overwhelmed by the pomp and splendour of the Vatican. The Swiss Guards in their slashed uniforms of yellow and blue standing with halberds at the doors; the papal police in black busbies and white breeches – one always wonders how they ever get into those big patent leather boots that come up nearly to their thighs. Then the Noble Guard at the doors of the Antechamber. Even in their ordinary uniform of blue and gold they look resplendent, but one should see them on a festal day. Top boots, white breeches and scarlet coats, topped by a helmet burnished like the sun and down behind from the peak of the helmet the tail of a horse so black that it must come from the wild Tartar steppes.

87

It is customary to say that all popes are charming, and because they are Christ's Vicar on earth that they are holy and wise. They can be all these things and yet one may not see it.

I do not ever remember seeing any man in which God's kindly light shone so truly as in the present pope. He is lovely. He looks thin, worn and old and yet he moves with the grace of a bird. He gives you the impression that he is not of this world at all, that somehow he has just come and may not stay long. When he speaks he has a soft mellow voice and you know that he is gentle and kind. I am glad God gave me the grace to see him, because I prayed for him all through the war.

The Father General brought him round and introduced each member of the Chapter to him. He asked me where I worked and I told him. I begged him a special blessing for all the members of our three societies and for all who help in our work, and he freely gave it.

"I give you a special blessing," he said, "because of the Father General."

Well, you all share in this, my dear members, and I send his blessing to you, as it came to me.

Carmelite News September-October 1947.

It was just as well that Elias was no longer responsible for the parish because demands on his ability to fund projects grew. From Dublin he was being asked to help with a new student house and the founding of the missions in Rhodesia (Zimbabwe) while nearer to home the situation in Aberystwyth was problematic. If Saint Mary's was to continue as a junior seminary it would have to fulfil a host of regulations which were impossible to implement on the site in Aberystwyth. A new property was purchased some sixty miles to the south east at Llandeilo. The property, a fine house, was set in a hundred acres of land. It was near the main road into England and had good rail connections. The cost of purchase and setting up the new college was £30,000. The college was opened on September 24th 1947 with Bishop Petit of Menevia celebrating Mass. The fact that the college was open within nine months of purchase is a

Pope Pius XII

tribute to immense hard work by Malachy and Pat Geary. The post-war years were times of shortage and so any building maintenance work cost time and energy seeking permits and chasing scarce materials. Elias spelt out costings in his newsletters, and while the sums could look small to us, £500 in the late-1940s would be the equivalent of £25,000 at the start of the twenty-first century. However, at the end of it all there was a sigh of relief and evidently the bank manager was confident that the debt would be paid. Elias was blunt in his approach: could ten thousand recipients of his newsletter send £1 apiece!

89

The Carmelite friary at Llandeilo.

One detail that Elias attended to was the provision of statues for the chapel at Llandeilo. How he went about it says something about his sensitivity, and also the artist he chose – along with his son Michael – was to have a long and creative association with the Carmelite Friars.

Well, there you have six statues. One thing I was determined on. I would not buy these statues out of a repository, so I gave a commission to Mr. Lindsay Clark who is one of the outstanding Catholic sculptors in England. He has turned these statues out of wood. He was about to be demobilised from the Royal Air Force. I had met him often while he was stationed in Sheppey in command of the R.A.F. regiment there. We agreed that he should undertake this commission when he was free. It has now been done. Six statues at £60 each. Didn't he have a job getting the wood! In the end he had to buy the timbers of old Thames barges. He nearly broke his back trying to carve them, because the wood was hundreds of years old and as hard as iron. Here and there he had to plug the holes where the ships' carpenters had driven the wooden pins that held the barges together.

One day I came upon him in his studio sitting upon an upturned box wiping the sweat from his brow, and his salutation to me was, "Oh Lord, I have loved the beauty of Thy house – but I never deserved this!" I consoled him. Mr. Lindsay Clark is very modern; maybe I ought to use the French word and say *moderne*. His interpretation of Saint Teresa would not please everyone, but somehow or other I have come to the conclusion that we must meet these modern artists at least half way. I realise that what the average person wants is the smiling and beautiful statue of Saint Teresa that is seen in shop windows, but the artist won't have that. We must allow the artist to give us what he thinks is a better interpretation of Saint Teresa. If we agree with the artist we shall at least get something different, but if we go on taking what is in the shop window we will in the end be appalled by the multitude of similitude. Anyway, I side with the artist. On the other hand I don't expect everyone to agree either with me or with the artist. Some of our pious people would see no connection between the statue and the photograph of Saint Teresa and reject

91

it as an imposture. I think it is going to be very difficult for saints that are born into a photographic age. I would not feel nervous about putting this statue of the Little Flower by Mr. Lindsay Clark in a pubic church, although popular taste in statues of the Little Flower likes to see the familiar picture changed into wood. I see many good reasons why I should put these statues in a college chapel. There they will serve the purpose of educating our students to appreciate something that is better than the shop window tradition. It costs money! Six statues at £60 each costs £360. Is there anyone sufficiently interested in the matter to present one of these statues to the chapel in Llandeilo?

Carmelite News May-June 1947.

The statue of Saint Thérèse by Philip Lindsey Clark (1889-1977).

A highlight for Elias was a visit to America in the autumn of 1948. He received an invitation to preach in New York from Donald O'Callaghan, a Carmelite who was a well-known figure in Irish-American circles. Elias travelled to America on the liner *America* which sailed from Southampton and called at Cobh, a port that had seen so many leave Ireland never to return. It was a rough crossing but not without sociable moments. What struck Elias was not just the skyscrapers but the contrasts:

> It is a city of violent contrasts – civilisation and the jungle, extreme wealth and grinding poverty. You could starve and fall down from hunger on the sidewalks, you could lie and be shovelled into a garbage can and few would care. Yet starving Europe could be fed from what Americans leave on their plates.

American food was not to his taste chiefly because it was so tasteless. He was charmed by some of the glitz but time and again he was aware that in England and Ireland the poor get a better deal. His summing up of the police while in a jocular vein again pointed up the contrasts: "The cops are a tough lot, revolvers and truncheons! They shoot first and apologise to your relatives (if any) afterwards."

Elias had a chance to see the mid-West and California, and yet at the end he was glad to be back in England's green and pleasant land. One of his comments about Irish-Americans rings true. "Few of them could live in Ireland again. The pace of life in America is too fast and one must walk at the pace one had learned."

Soon after his return from America Elias was to be involved in negotiations that would lead to the purchase of *The Friars* in Aylesford and enable the Order to return to its medieval home. One of the reasons why Father John Cogan was ready to accept the offer of a foothold in Kent in 1926 was the fact that Faversham and Sittingbourne were near to Aylesford. During the reign of James II the Prior General of the day petitioned the king for the return of the priory but to no avail. Now there was a hope that one day the Carmelites

93

might return. In fact as early as 1929 Elias Magennis and Malachy visited *The Friars* wanting to see what the old priory looked like. They were graciously received by the Copely Hewitts, the owners at that time, and perhaps a bond was forged. The Copely Hewitts cared for *The Friars* but by the end of the war the effort of maintaining the property was beyond them. Once *The Friars* was on the market it needed swift action by the Order. Fortunately Elias was well placed not just because of his being in Faversham but through his contacts in the county. Obviously he had the support of his brother Kilian, now Prior General. Kilian, with his American connections, was able to raise money in the States but the negotiations needed someone on the ground to ensure that the Carmelites should succeed. By the summer of 1949 *The Friars* was in Carmelite hands again and the Prior General appointed his brother Malachy as the first Prior. Malachy was just fifty at this time with a wide range

This painting by Adam Kossowski, depicting the return of the friars to Aylesford, hangs in the Prior's Hall. It features Brother Anthony carrying the cross, followed by Kilian Lynch, who faces his brother Malachy. Elias Lynch is shown in his glasses and Carmelite skull-cap.

94

of pastoral experience and well tested in managing projects and buildings, but above all he had a sense of what was appropriate and could recognise giftedness in others. If he had any shortcoming it was perhaps a lack of what could seem like realism in financial matters, an approach that could irritate Elias and would do in years to come.

Elias was delighted with the acquisition of *The Friars* and for the next three years was able to give the work of re-founding considerable support. 'The Return of the Carmelites' took place on 31ˢᵗ October 1949 but in the weeks before a great deal of practical work was done. Elias ensured that despite the restrictions of rationing all involved in 'The Return' were fed and watered and, to the best of his ability, kept warm.

The role of Aylesford in the Order's life was to be one that evolved rather than flowed from a grand plan. Local clergy hoped it would be the site of a school; Rome saw it as a centre for studies; but popular reaction took it down the path of being a centre of pilgrimage. It was seen as being connected with the 'Scapular Vision' of Our Lady to the medieval Carmelite Saint Simon Stock, and the return of the relics of Simon Stock in 1951 fixed that direction, one that would bring financial and practical implications.

However, Elias saw the acquisition of Aylesford in more than practical terms and saw a return to our origins as helping the Order to really feel at home again in England. "History", he wrote, "is a mighty thing. It is good for men to stand where their fathers stood before them and to look back over four hundred years of English life and to be able to say, "Here is where we left off". Tradition too is a wonderful thing. It is a silent yet active thing that works in the minds of men. It will work in the minds of future Carmelites telling them that they must never cease to preach devotion to Mary and make Aylesford once more her shrine." [*Newsletter* September-October 1949.] This vision of tradition, continuity and hope for the future was one that Elias shared with Malachy and there was also a sense that the nightmare of persecution and prejudice was coming to an end for Catholics. It is not easy for Roman Catholics in the twenty-first century to

95

realise how Britain, even in the 1940s, was still in many ways inhospitable to Catholicism. Events like the return of the friars to Aylesford were welcomed green shoots.

For the next two years raising funds and supporting Aylesford was high on Elias's list of priorities. Yet by now his health was becoming problematic with the onset of diabetes and despite being a big man he was vulnerable to infections like bronchitis. He was well aware that the buildings at Aylesford needed radical repairs and adequate facilities if they were to welcome pilgrims. The proposed return of the relics of Saint Simon Stock in the summer of 1951 gave an added urgency and a tight timetable. Along with Brother Anthony, Elias devised new ways of raising money to support the efforts already being made by Malachy. Elias commented on the problems they expected but added that his expectations were surpassed! Essential services had to be relayed, gas, water and electricity all had to be renewed at a cost, but at least the place was safe and supplies were assured. Roofs had to be repaired and the neglect caused by the war years put to rights. What had served as stables and stores were restored to serve as accommodation for pilgrims, while kitchens and toilets were needed. The Pilgrims' Hall was made good to serve pilgrims for meals and that essential cup of tea. In among the appeals is a sentence that could be overlooked. *"Future plans include the building of a first class secondary school for the district."* [*Newsletter* September-October 1950.] This was never to be, though the concept was raised again in 1955, but by then Elias was to see this as too little too late. However, what was also in Elias's mind and perhaps something the Prior General dreamt of was a place where the traditions and spirituality of the Order could be pursued.

The return of the relics of Saint Simon Stock was a magnificent success and by the autumn of that year it became clear that Elias was no longer able to give time and raise money for Aylesford. The reasons for his attitude were in the end practical and based on realism. It was obvious that the development at Aylesford was going to involve large sums of money over a long period. At the same time the Order in Britain was at a crossroads as the Prior General

96

The Pilgrims' Hall at Aylesford.

The relic of Saint Simon Stock being brought to Aylesford in 1951.

97

wanted the communities to be independent of Ireland under a local Provincial Superior who in this case was to be Father Patrick Geary. Elias realised that his energies were needed to provide adequate financial support for this venture. He makes a statement of intent in the autumn newsletter of 1951.

Fr. Patrick Geary, O.Carm.

Well having said all that let us get back to the work our societies are designed to do. The support of our students and the organisation of the material resources of our missions is the main object of our work. We will be talking to you in the future more about this than <u>anything else</u>.

Elias Lynch (centre) celebrating the return of the Carmelite friars to Aylesford Priory on the eve of All Saints, 1949, accompanied by Councillor H. Knowles, J.P., Mayor of Faversham (left), and Alderman Phil Johnson, O.B.E., J.P. (right).

99

The next few years were to be hectic times of tension making many demands but not without a lighter side. It was about this time that Elias was to suffer something of an upset in his public life. He had been a town councillor in Faversham for fourteen years and had given time and energy to that role. As Chairman of Housing he had ensured that a good stock of council houses were built to meet the needs of post-war Faversham. This was an achievement that was long remembered. So it seemed proper that he should exercise the role of Mayor; however, with everything in place disaster struck as in the local elections Elias lost his seat and with it the chance to be Mayor. It would seem that Elias, while an Independent, was viewed with hostility by sections of the Labour Party and on the day of the election an item in the local press was to prove his undoing. Labour councillors accused Elias as Chair of Housing of neglecting property in West Street and allowing infestation by rats. The story lost him votes and his seat. It must have been a hard blow, but doubtless his resilient humour enabled him to cope with unforeseen rejection. Some twenty years later another Carmelite, Gregory Fitzgerald, became Mayor of Lampeter, a tribute to his commitment to the local community.

About this time Elias issued a manifesto stating that he would never ask for money but he would tell the world what he was trying to do and if there was the good will to help he would be thankful. He also reminded his readers of the wisdom of making a will and perhaps making a bequest or leaving the residue to the Carmelite charity. Money was needed to enable the College at Aberystwyth to develop its work as a centre where late vocations to the priesthood could do their preliminary training. Many of the men who went to Aberystwyth proceeded to ordination, some becoming Carmelites. Novices for the newly-established Province were based at Aylesford and already a number of students were studying in Rome. Besides all this the Prior General asked for help with a project in Fatima, Portugal. In among all this pragmatic activity there were hopes like establishing a House of Studies in Cambridge. It's no wonder that Elias sometimes dreamt of going off to be a hermit in the wilds of Scotland.

100

Whatever the disappointments, Elias was often surprised by people's generosity and humanity. He writes of one such encounter.

A few weeks ago I had a most enjoyable interlude. A nice old lady from Bolton in Lancashire came along to see us. She travelled to London by bus and reached Faversham late one night. Under her arm she had a brown paper parcel and she was most anxious to see me before she would confide herself to such hospitality as could be found in the town. Well, we found her a comfortable billet. The next morning she told us why she had come. She had worked hard all her life, she had never married, and being a very intelligent woman, she had made some money. Having no children of her own she wished to have a child in God. In other words, she wished to educate a young man for the priesthood in the Carmelite Order. To my surprise, she produced the best part of £1,000 and handed it over as gaily as if we were doing her a favour.

It is always a pleasure to talk to people from Lancashire. The bluff, hearty, honest way they speak to you; they say what they have to say and expect you to do the same. When I asked her under whose name I should found the burse, she immediately named Saint Martha the patroness of priests' housekeepers, housewives, nurses, clippies, police women and waitresses. In other words, Saint Martha, in her mind, is the patroness of all women who work for a living and just get that, the women whose work begins in the early morning and finishes late at night. What a marvellous idea for a burse! Because our literature goes to nearly every Presbytery in England, Scotland and Wales. She told me that the particular devotion to Saint Martha consisted in praying to her, and secondly, on lighting a candle in honour of Saint Martha every Tuesday. I asked her, "Why Tuesday?" She said, "Parish priests are usually away on Monday, and there's no trouble in the house."

Carmelite News December-January 1953. Saint Martha's Burse.

101

Elias always had a love of Lancashire folk remembering the warm welcome he received when he had gone north to preach on Mary and Thérèse.

By the 1950s travel was becoming easier; it was possible to fly to Ireland and the Continent and Elias took advantage of these possibilities. He obviously enjoyed a visit to Barcelona in 1952 and left a picture of a way of life that fifty years on would be hard to reproduce.

> It is a lovely city, so vibrantly alive that one can feel it in the walk and conversation of the people. They are small, graceful, proud and courteous. If you bump into one of them, all you do is to raise your hat and smile and look suitably sorry. Their faces light up and they smile and say, "It is a pleasure."
>
> The food is good and plentiful, but expensive. It is a high pleasure to sit and chew small green olives over a glass of sherry before lunch.
>
> What a joy it is to eat fish that has been cooked with some respect for the fish!
>
> The Catalonian men have sleek black hair and frizzy eyebrows, which must surely come from the coffee which they drink – the blackest, bitterest brew ever poured into a cup. They have a profound respect for their own feet, and wear shoes as fanciful as those of the ladies.
>
> Shoe-shining is a trade. If you sit at a café table, you may find a shoe shiner cleaning your shoes because he takes it for granted that they need shining. It costs only sixpence. First they clean the leather and shine with a cloth, and then they anoint the shoes with liquid polish and shine them with a brush. They finish them by rubbing wax over the surface with their hands, and a quick rub of a cloth brings up a shine like the "Waves of Tory".
>
> There is a vegetable market somewhere around here and the farmers come in with their produce in covered carts. They are brown, hairy, sturdy little men and every man has his pipe. Every cart has its little black and white dog. There he sits on top of the load knowing full well that he owns it, and that it is his job to guard it – and guard it he does! If anyone goes near to the cart, he makes it completely evident that he is quite prepared to eat

them alive. They are very intelligent. They know the traffic lights and the hand signals of the traffic cops, and if the driver doesn't move fast enough, they jump down beside him barking like mad, as much as to say, "What are you thinking about. Get a move on!" The dogs live on the carts all their lives. They are fed only by their masters. Sometimes they develop a great affection for the horse or mule with which they travel and sometimes they die of grief when master travels on.

The churches are beautiful, dark, rich, ornate and never empty. They seem to resent the light of the sun, and the gold and silver of the altars gleam from the light of the candles like bright tapestries in the moonlight. In every church I saw, there is an altar to Our Lady of Mount Carmel and the Holy Souls. She is the Universal Consolatrix in life and death. There is no scarcity of holy souls – dozens of them and always a few clergy and nuns. It is nice to know this.

There is no Society for the Prevention of Cruelty to Children in Spain. It has never been necessary. The whole street would stop to ask why a child was crying. In fact the children are in charge. They chatter, chirrup, sing and boss their parents and the parents enjoy it. That maybe is the reason why the Spaniards are so proud. They have never been kicked around.

Tibidabo is a mountain just outside Barcelona. As you go up the long, tree-lined avenues you can see it straight ahead. The Spaniards are building a National Thanksgiving Church right on top of it – in fact two churches, one on top of the other. Tibidabo means "I will give you" from the words of Christ. It is their way of saying "Thanks."

The picture "Our Lady of Fatima" is being shown in the most luxurious cinema in Barcelona.

I move on this afternoon to hard-faced France. It has been a pleasure to meet a people so highly civilised.

Carmelite News December-January 1952. Barcelona.

The autumn newsletter of 1953 had two announcements of importance and both had an implication for the other. A brief section of the letter said that a

103

shrine could be built with the order to wait on more news with bated breath. On the back page there was a longer piece headed "Delbridge House".

We have purchased Delbridge House at the top of Preston Street, Faversham, as a future Guest House for the parish.

Many members of our Societies wish to pay a visit to Faversham, and it is difficult to get accommodation for them. We are fixing up Delbridge House so that it will be clean and comfortable. There will be an excellent kitchen and dining room and a soft drinks department. The guest house will cater both for the residential and recreational needs of the visitors. We hope that

THE CARMELITE NEWS

FRONTAGE VIEW OF DELBRIDGE HOUSE

We send our thanks to all our clients who lent us money to defray the capital expenses of conversion, and the loans will be repaid promptly one year after the date of acceptance.

Delbridge House has created great excitement in Faversham. The membership is already over 400. I am convinced that it will become the Mecca of the town. It will create a bridge between Catholic and non-Catholic — a forum in which both sides can meet. From time to time in the "Carmelite News" we will print shots of the interior. Thanks to all. It has been a very fine job.

We wish to thank also the people who sent books for the library, and these were many. We were not able to thank all that sent books personally, because in some cases the names were not included. We would like also, to thank those who lent money without interest.

From September 1st 1954 onwards, there will be a Guest House under Catholic management connected with the Shrine of St. Jude. Six bed-sitting rooms, full or partial board Apply Secretary, "Uplees" 13, Newton Road, Faversham Kent

Delbridge House as it appeared in the Carmelite News, September-October 1954.

it will be patronised by rambling clubs, hikers and cycling clubs from the Home Counties. Moreover, we intend to develop it as an International Centre for students, preferably of the University type. This has long been a great need of this town. I have persuaded my superiors to advance me the purchase money but I am landed with the costs of conversion. Would any of our readers like to lend me the necessary money in units of £50 or £100 at 3%? It would be a short term loan to be repaid within two years. The security is excellent. The name of the place will not be changed because it is perhaps the best known house in Faversham. It is a large old Georgian House with a beautiful staircase. We have over an acre of ground at the back. It is right beside the railway station and beside the main bus stops. All buses in and out of Faversham stop just outside. This is of course, highly important – to get people there and to get them away again is one of the first needs of a recreational centre. We are now right on the hub of things as far as that goes.

The various activities carried on there will be a focal centre for the Catholics of the town and I think that with a wise management it will be a great asset to Catholic social life.

Any valuer whose opinion I have asked reckons that the house and grounds attached is worth £8,500 as it stands. I bought it for £2,250 as it stands. If you ask me the reason why I have been able to buy it at that price, all I can say is, that Faversham is a small town and it was a little too big for local users. It will not be parish property but will have the support of the Order.

Carmelite News September-October 1953. Delbridge House.

Delbridge House was close by the railway station; a fine eighteenth-century building. Elias could see the logic of the deal but many of his confreres were puzzled. However in all these dealings – and there were many excursions into property – Elias had the trust of his Provincial Superior whom he kept informed at all times with care and courtesy. Besides that, Elias had a network of business contacts whose advice was sound. Delbridge House was up and running within a year and among the aspirations Elias hoped it would create

105

a bridge between Catholic and non-Catholic; a forum in which both sides could meet. I have memories of Delbridge House in the 1950s; a welcoming place, and one feature that struck me was the large-screen T.V., a piece of what then seemed avant-garde technology. Another memory was a birthday party with Elias urging us on to enjoy ourselves. His sister Mary Halpin was there; the youngest of the family who enjoyed engaging her big brother in verbal duels which would end in honourable draws. One of Elias's nephews Kilian

---

Tariff
Delbridge House
Faversham, Kent
HOSTEL AND CLUB

Telephone 2942   Manager: Mr. L. Reed.

BOARD RESIDENCE
Board per week … £7
Bed and Breakfast … 12s.6d.

MEALS FOR NON-RESIDENTS
Breakfast … 3s.0d.
Lunch … 3s.6d. to 4s.0d.
Afternoon tea … 2s.0d.
Dinner … 6s.6d

MORNING COFFEE, HIGH TEA, SUPPERS

CHILDREN
A reduction is made for children.
Half-rate under 6 years (if not taking late dinner).
Up to 10 years, two thirds rate.
Special reduced rates for cycling clubs.

106

Halpin would keep me company and fifty years on we share vivid memories. The management of Delbridge House was another task for Elias and at times, despite his enthusiasm, it could be an added concern especially in the staffing of the place. A list of prices from those days reminds us of inflation over the last half century.

As if the building of the shrine and opening Delbridge House were not enough, Elias was also expanding the press. In that context he was off to Düsseldorf for the international exhibition of printing machinery. His reactions show interest in the whole business of printing and his amazement at technical marvels.

However, by the spring of 1954 Elias was ready to launch the building of the shrine to Saint Jude. Elias had wanted to build this shrine for many years as devotion to the apostle – who is seen as patron of those who struggle and feel hopeless – had grown during the war years.

Interior of the Shrine of Saint Jude shortly after construction.

107

During the war Elias found a Spanish sixteenth-century statue of the apostle and the donor who helped purchase the statue believed he was giving it to Faversham in memory of his son "missing presumed dead". However, before the statue could reach Faversham the young man was found to be a prisoner of war.

*The sixteenth-century Spanish statue of Saint Jude
in front of the mosaic at the shrine by Michael Leigh.*

CARM

By 1954 it was possible to get the necessary licences and permits so that the building of the shrine could begin. Elias announced that he had found an artist, Michael Leigh, who had produced a design of great dignity. The shrine would not be very big and expensive but it would be beautiful. Elias saw it as austere and simple, achieving its effect from good planning and lighting. As the shrine was being built Brother Anthony hit on an ingenious way of raising money. Donors were allowed to lay a brick for one shilling. Evidently visitors from Lancashire were most forthcoming and Elias always liked to hear the mellow accent. He was pleased that visitors from other churches came along to handle the trowel and help with the building.

Mary, mother of Jesus, overshadowed by the Holy Spirit.
Window by Richard Joseph King at the shrine of Saint Jude.

109

The artists who worked on the shrine came with their expertise. Michael Leigh was recognised for his mosaics, Anthony Foster was an established sculptor and Richard King provided powerful stained glass windows of Carmelite saints. Adam Kossowski had also left his mark with his distinctive ceramics.

Finally Elias was able to acquire a sixteenth-century Flemish reliquary for as little as £500, a fitting home for the relic of Saint Jude. All in all, the project moved ahead quickly and on 28th October 1955 Archbishop Cowderoy of Southwark dedicated the shrine, assisted by the Prior General and the Prior

The reliquary of Saint Jude at the shrine in Faversham.

110

of Aylesford. The Archbishop was delighted with the new shrine and the three Lynch brothers came together to celebrate, perhaps remembering their days as servers in that country chapel.

Writing in the summer of 1955, just before the blessing, Elias showed how the newly acquired Delbridge House could serve as accommodation for pilgrims. Obviously this project was dear to his heart and his deep desire for sociability.

Delbridge House is not just a club; it is one of the smartest places in North East Kent. It is owned by the Carmelites, by a Board of Trustees of the priests of the Order. The management is Catholic and it is residential. It has, I think the smartest bar and dining room in North East Kent, and one thing that is not provided in normal places, a Ladies' Powder Room that will beat comparison with any hotel on the South Coast.

You may think it queer to have me talking like this, but I am an old soldier and I have come to the conclusion that nothing is <u>too good</u> for <u>Catholics</u>; and another thing, we have got to show outsiders that we are <u>smarter</u> than they are, and that we have <u>no lessons</u> to learn from them.

Delbridge House has a small and smart dining room; 25 to 30 people. A fine hall where you have facilities for music and dancing, and above all, toilet facilities for men and women that are quite out of the ordinary provision. But we can cater for groups of over 100.

You may wonder why I do this. Alright, I have done it at great sacrifice. I have done it because I believe that Catholics should set a headline and show other people how things ought to be done in social recreation. Come along and try it! We have a Guest House in case you may think there is an overflow. Our Guest House is just as smart as the rest.

It's no harm to blow one's own horn occasionally. <u>God be with you</u>.

Carmelite News May-June 1955

111

The sentiments he expresses can seem odd today but they are a reminder of how fifty years ago the Catholic community still lived in the shadow of the Penal Days. There was still an attitude in society that could make Catholics feel outsiders in their own country. Ecumenism has changed the landscape but occasionally it is still possible to stumble on latent prejudices.

While so much was happening at Faversham Elias was also involved in the work of establishing the Anglo-Welsh Province and was all too conscious of problems at Aylesford with his brother ill and, in Elias's eyes, not realistic.

Now that the Carmelite friars in England and Wales were on their way to being an independent Province of the Order the question of forming those who wanted to join the brothers arose. The immediate solution had been to start a novitiate for new friars at Aylesford and then send the newly professed to Rome for their studies. However, Elias was soon drawn into projects about relocating the novitiate. Elias thought Allington Castle – a Carmelite community near Aylesford – would be ideal, but Malachy saw it as a home for his newly founded *Institute of Our Lady of Mount Carmel*. Attention then switched to Hartley near Dartford where the friars were caring for a parish and a shrine to Our Lady. There was land available for building and Hartley had good road and rail links. There was talk of building accommodation for some twenty friars and the proposal was to ask Gilbert Scott, the architect of Liverpool Cathedral, to design the project. Elias envisaged a single story building with the chapel and refectory at the heart of the complex. In his mind's eye he was dreaming of something that would evoke the desert, the eremitical life of the first Carmelite hermits. Elias wrote to Pat Geary, "I rather like the idea of each student having his own separate little cell on a strung out basis. It would be unique in novitiates of religious orders in Britain … I don't think that we ought to bother too much about the £50,000 cost." Nothing more came of the project though the location of the novitiate continued to be a topic of discussion among the friars in Britain over the years.

1955 saw Elias trying to sort out the practicalities of separating his fundraising for the Order at large from the local parish finances. Originally his fundraising

had been a way of surviving in Faversham; now the reality was different with the parish becoming self-sufficient. The parish was cared for by a young friar, Camillus Lawler, and Elias wanted him to use his energies to build up the parish. Elias saw that the church was in good repair and was encouraging the local Catholic community to be generous. However, another factor in the setting up of new structures was a difficulty in relationships between Elias and some of the younger friars who came to Faversham. Perhaps it was a generation gap, the fact that some of these men were not communicative, or perhaps they could well have felt over-awed living alongside a man who in many ways was becoming a legend in his own life time.

Besides events at Faversham, difficulties at Aylesford began to preoccupy Elias. Years of hard work and neglect of his diabetes were taking their toll on Malachy's health. Just after New Year in 1955 Malachy collapsed and had to be hospitalized and spend time in convalescence. Elias had gone over in the middle of the night to anoint his brother who seemed in danger of death. Malachy was so ill that he was unaware that his condition was so serious, with no recollection of how close to death he had been.

By the spring Malachy was back at Aylesford, yet feeling overwhelmed by financial problems arising from the restoration work. The overdraft was approaching £25,000 so desperate measures were the order of the day. On top of all this Malachy felt utterly exhausted, aware that all of these pressures were coming on top of his illness.

Among the ideas that were floated was the sale of Allington Castle to Lord Bossom, who was at that time member of parliament for Maidstone. Malachy hoped to sell the Castle for £40,000 and move the sisters who lived there to the farmhouse at Aylesford. The other plan was to turn the newly built workshops and accommodation into a school.

None of these proposals came to anything, Lord Bossom had no intention of paying £40,000 for Allington and the Prior General was against the sale, while the idea of starting a school was to fade from view.

113

Elias was to write about these events in a letter of April 6th 1955 to Pat Geary, the Provincial Superior.

> "I think we will have to be careful about Malachy – ideas are tumbling through his head at such a rate that one is in danger of knocking the other out. You know how I fought in the beginning for a school at Aylesford and it sounds so strange that he should come round to the idea now it's too late."

Elias went on to say that Aylesford needed a business committee to manage the project so that no one person could incur unmanageable debts. Elias, while willing to take risks, was careful enough to assess the risk. He was vocal in opposing the situation at Aylesford fearing that "the whole mess will be unloaded on us". Despite some set backs the work of restoring Aylesford did not hit the rocks and by 1958 the work of building the shrine was underway with Sir Adrian Scott as architect. Allington Castle was to know some uncertain moments but it was to remain in Carmelite hands until the end of the twentieth century. Elias would continue to be annoyed by his brother's activities and a letter of September 1957 shows him in combative mood as he lets off steam to Pat Geary. The cause of his annoyance was Malachy sending out leaflets in honour of Saint Jude, thus cutting across the work of Faversham. Elias fumed to Pet Geary, "If we allow Aylesford to muscle in on the Saint Jude devotion you will have a penniless Province on your hands. Aylesford is a very practical example of catch a penny piety."

Elias admired Pat Geary and was a loyal confrere, supporting him and enabling him to get on with the growth of the Province. The Province was growing in numbers with a steady flow of vocations and about this time money was raised to buy a property at Cheltenham that would enable a new school to open. Pat Geary as Provincial Superior was very much involved in this development which was to have its share of difficulties. Elias did all he could to help Pat, especially when the toughness of the situation began to take its toll. Elias ensured that money was not a problem, negotiated with the lawyers, and gave his confrere of his time and his sympathy. The school, Whitefriars, at Charlton Kings on the Oxford side of Cheltenham, opened and was successful. However the problems that attended the setting up of Whitefriars and the legal tussles that ensued affected Pat Geary's health, and for a while Elias had to step into the breach as Provincial Superior. He was well able to hold things together, though by now at just over sixty he seemed an old man. Like most of his family Elias was affected by diabetes and again years of responsibility were beginning to tell. He was more than happy, in late 1959, to hand over responsibility to a new Provincial Superior, Conleth Fitzgerald, an old friend and a jovial but shrewd Kerry man. About this time Elias's younger brother Kilian finished his time as Prior General and became Prior of Aylesford. Elias could relax and know that Aylesford was in safe hands.

Life at Faversham was more peaceful as Barry Cogan was parish priest. Barry was a kind, generous man who understood Elias, and apart from occasional contretemps with the housekeeper life was on a reasonably even keel, that is apart from burglars. Just before Christmas 1959 a serious break-in cost Faversham some hundreds of pounds and what was galling was that Rex the Alsatian dog – normally fierce – slept though the whole episode!

This was a time of change which Elias found encouraging. John XXIII was Pope. John F. Kennedy was President of the United States and in Russia Khrushchev was making waves. Life in England was less austere under the benign auspices of Harold McMillan the Prime Minister who reminded the nation that they had "never had it so good!"

By 1960 Elias was in the autumn of his life. He had lived in Faversham long enough to be part of the town's fabric and he was renowned for his generosity and kindness. When he was Chair of the Housing Committee he delighted in ensuring young families got a house and no one came to the door without receiving help. He preferred to be duped rather than send anyone away empty-handed. His kindness inspired loyalty. An elderly lady spoke to me of Elias driving her to hospital during a blizzard way back in 1940; years later her gratitude was undiminished. A shy man in many ways, Elias had a

115

gift for friendship with a wide variety of people: Princess Andrew Romanov, the novelist Kate O'Brien, the Ardizzone family, and countless colleagues in business and local politics. Birthdays were done in style and when a new vicar of Saint Mary Charity arrived in the mid-1950s a welcoming reception was organized in Delbridge House. He also enjoyed welcoming fellow Carmelites to enjoy the hospitality at Whitefriars. However, there was one rule never to be transgressed: never criticize another member of Elias's family. Elias could criticize his brothers, but if you endorsed the criticism the door was shown. More than one Carmelite was to find their stay in Faversham come to a sudden end. Yet Elias was fond of his confreres, especially those who rejoiced in an amount of nonconformity. One of these was Michael O'Carroll. Michael was immensely gifted but sadly often subverted his cause. However, he had great gifts as a poet with what Elias called, "a genuine touch, something that stands beside Yeats – a gift for diction and a graciousness of word seldom found today."

Despite the onset of ill health Elias loved to travel, be it back to Ireland or over to Europe, often enjoying the hospitality of the Marymount nuns who over the years forged strong links with the Carmelites in London, Paris and Rome, among other places. Elias loved to capture the atmosphere of wherever he stayed, having a strong romantic streak along with a love of nature and a vivid imagination.

The last years of his life saw a radical decline in his health, and yet despite times when he nearly died he kept working away, writing the Faversham newsletter, travelling and playing his part in the life of the Province. He was fortunate to have a loyal secretary in Diane Farrell, and friends who helped him travel when failing eyesight made driving impossible. 1960 saw him hospitalized with an ulcer that would not heal because of his diabetes. This left him at death's door, and yet writing about the episode he composed a eulogy about the nursing profession.

I am convinced that the nursing profession is one of the noblest of all. A girl who devotes her life to nursing is a great benefactor of humanity. I will never cease to sing the praises of the nursing staff who have looked after me since my operation.

When I came into hospital I weighed nearly fourteen stone, and after my operation I was completely helpless; yet these little people turned me around, rolled me over and bandaged me four times a day. They persuaded me that I was getting better when everyone thought I was going to die. Where they found strength to do what they did, I do not know. No one could say that nursing is a pleasant job. It is not. It is hard and unrelenting. The human body is a poor thing and when it has been cut about by surgeons only nurses can bring it back to active life again. I shall never forget them.

You know you get an entirely new view of women when you are lying helpless on your back and all you can do is look up at them. I made up my mind that I would write a booklet one day and that the title of it would be "Looking up at them". You realize that you are completely at their mercy and that you must trust your life to their loyalty and devotion to their profession. They were quite a mixture. There were English, Irish and some Scotch, but one thing made a great impression on me and that is how wonderful an asset the gift of faith is to any girl who is a nurse, because there are times when she is working only for the love of God. Then, and always, I think that their ministry is not merely a help but a blessing as well.

Carmelite News June-August 1960. A noble profession.

About this time Brother Anthony was also ill. He had cancer, but after surgery it seemed he was in reasonable health. Over the years Anthony had masterminded the organization of the newsletter and had taken much of the burden of administration off Elias's shoulders. He was also a loyal and caring confrere and although the two of them could have their differences they were close friends. However, Anthony, despite care and attention, never fully recovered and by 1965 it was obvious he had secondary cancers and by June he had died. He and Elias had been together for thirty years. Elias described his feelings: "an old friendship, sometimes erratic, but underneath it was a great respect between him and me – my personal worry is Anthony, because if he folds up it will be the end of a period." Perhaps if Anthony had heard these comments he would have replied with his laconic hallmark phrase "Is that so?!"

About this time Kilian, Elias's youngest brother, became the Provincial Superior. Kilian was the most austere of the three Carmelite brothers; disciplined, intellectual and full of energy. As Prior General he had brought new life to the Order, and while at heart kindly he has a steely resolve. One of his first acts was to make Elias give up his car, a Rover Three Litre. Elias enjoyed the comfort and style of the vehicle and felt the car suggested in its place was too much of a come down, "a mechanical perambulator" in his view. However Kilian was too wise to interfere on other issues. Kilian did appoint an ideal friar to fill the gap left by Anthony's death. Conleth Doyle, who was guest-master at Aylesford, had a sound business sense and a quiet sense of humour, qualities needed to fill the gap.

While Elias struggled with bad health he was always concerned about Malachy's welfare. At the beginning of 1966 Elias was struggling to recover from complications following an umbilical hernia operation. He needed blood transfusions and the situation was made worse by his diabetes. He said at the time, "I feel like a dying fish in the bottom of the barrel."

By the summer he was well enough to travel to Ireland, a chance to catch up with his family and see Carmelite confreres in Dublin. He was also anxious about Malachy who was convalescing at Dalkey near Dublin. Malachy was evidently not too happy about developments at Aylesford and Allington. Elias told him, "Everything seems to be going well upon this side. For goodness sake do try to avoid the fatal delusion that if you are not driving the bus that it will surely fall into the ditch. The old Carmelite Order has lasted a long time, it has improved marvellously in my time and no doubt will improve even more marvellously in the future. Try to

118

learn a sense of detachment and try to do as I have learned to do, to sit in the back seat. It is a seat of honour; it gives you the ancient liberty of an elder to criticize the stupidities of the younger and if God gives you the grace to acknowledge it to see yourself in their mistakes, because surely you made the same mistakes in your time as they are making now." [June 6th 1966]. Sound advice for all of us to heed.

As 1967 progressed Elias began to look forward to his seventieth birthday. It was a real landmark and given his ever more precarious health it looked a little uncertain that he would see the day. He did reach it, and was able to celebrate the occasion with memorable lines in what was to be the last newsletter he was to write.

On September 25th I celebrated my seventieth birthday. In the religious life we hardly ever celebrate our birthdays, but it seemed to me that on that day I would be three score years and ten, that God would have given me grace to live so long. It isn't a long time perhaps in your estimation, but we are a short lived family; I think it is because we all had a bee in our bonnet and that eventually buzzed our lives away.

I have often wished God had sent a few normally stupid people into our large family; we numbered thirteen – nine brothers and four sisters. But he didn't. It was always very hard to talk to them because they could argue you into a coma. They were all too intelligent by a half. Their trouble was they never had the necessary background of scholastic education to be too clever about anything. However, over half of them are dead now; like the top of an old tree broken by the gales of time the few of us who are left do not look as brave as we would like.

So I thought that I would celebrate my seventieth birthday in case God was a little tired of seeing me around and would decide to take me away before my next Feast Day. Therefore I set my mind to worry out what I should do and the whole problem was settled for me by that nice old lady who wanted to give me a chalice and I started off a chalice fund by asking her to contribute £10. Some three hundred people subscribed to the fund and it was over

119

subscribed, so I had an extra idea – as I have mentioned before, our family were rich in ideas.

Carmelite News December 1967 - January 1968.
Three score and ten.

Elias Lynch celebrating Mass on his seventieth birthday.

In an impulse of generosity Elias found a beautiful Italian eighteenth-century chalice which he gave to Aylesford for concelebrations. However, within a few weeks of his seventieth birthday Elias was dead. He died in the Cottage Hospital in Faversham on All Saints Day, November 1st 1967.

His funeral was a celebration of a life of generosity and commitment. There was a large gathering of his family along with some forty of his Carmelite confreres. The Archbishop of Southwark presided at the requiem, calling Elias "one of the giants of our day". Kilian Healy, the Prior General, wrote "Only the Lord knows how hard he worked and how much he accomplished for the Order and the Church. May the young take inspiration from him and give themselves as he did for the Church in England – his adopted land."

Elias Lynch's grave marker at The Friars, Aylesford.

Portrait of Elias Lynch in Faversham by Michael Leigh.

Part 2

Letters to Cahal

In Part 1 of this book the story of Elias Lynch has to a great part been told in his own words. In this second section I would like his voice to be heard through the letters he wrote to Cahal in the 1960s and through some of his later *Carmelite Newsletters*. As I have inferred Elias was old for his years by the time he was in his sixties but his wit and wisdom did not falter.

Cahal – or Tommy – Gallagher (d. 1994) to whom the letters are addressed was some ten years younger than Elias, a warm-hearted but accident-prone person. Tommy stood for a warm human way of living the Carmelite *Rule* not always appreciated by the powers-that-be, but he always had a gentle touch in dealing with people. Elias felt that Tommy would have read his words with sympathy and perhaps issued the occasional challenge. However, we don't know if Tommy actually saw the letters.

Elias uses the letters to think aloud and express his hopes and fears. What does emerge is a love of the Carmelite Order which he sees as unpretentious and graced with a certain freedom.

At a time when living as a friar, monk or nun was viewed as strict, Elias rejoices in the ordinary, the relaxed, the really human. He also shows a genuine sense of valuing people as they are, realizing that all encounters are important, and

123

Fr. Cahal (Thomas) Gallagher, O.Carm.

some life changing. His reference to the role of the priest in the celebration of confession shows how sensitive he was in trying to be present and respectful to the people who came into his care.

Sometimes there is an evident frustration and impatience with life and those who would wish to organize us. However, without being pietistic Elias always found a resolution in seeking the will of God – carrying the Cross: "What better love would a Christian crave?"

Elias had a vivid imagination about the origins of the Carmelites and felt that the hermit element of the Order's vocation was stronger than people realized but not always expressed as one might expect. The hermit tendency could lead to individualism, but its positive side is a freedom from regimentation. While at times confreres obviously irritated Elias he was aware of his own awkwardness and that he could seem to intimidate when in reality he was nervous. Even though he gave of himself with immense energy he felt it was never enough, and so when he discovered he was diabetic he found a reason for his lack of vigour! He found what he saw as an awful debacle at Sittingbourne all of a piece with what could often be too gloomy a case of self assessment. Faversham, to begin with, was exile, and while he turned adversity into a creative apostolate he was always immensely self-conscious. He admitted that the memory of his struggle with life never left him and yet time and again he finds peace and resolution in seeking the will of God.

Besides his reflections on his life and ministry Elias enjoyed commenting on life in the round. The English temperament fascinated him and the Second World War gave rise to attitudes that he would tolerate with amused detachment.

One of his qualities was his ability to laugh at himself and the generous streak in his nature often led him to be taken for a ride. However, he was usually ready to give a woman the benefit of the doubt and showed no regret when he discovered duplicity. His generosity triggered vehemence when he encountered the mean and mistaken piety. He could never see the sense of imposed penances and rigidity; he realized life itself could provide times of testing.

Humour, love of nature and sometimes narratives that touch on the paranormal were also part of his repertoire. His tolerant acceptance of the blonde ladies and their nightly dealings with soldiers in Tanners Street shows a compassion that was of a piece with his generosity, even at a cost to his own convenience and his conscience.

125

Perhaps the overall impression that these pieces give is of a shrewd observer of life but also a constantly honest assessment of his own motives and inner life. His ability to turn a memorable phrase and evoke atmosphere flow from a person who kept a steady gaze on life but who never took himself too seriously. He loved nature and valued people, but always lived conscious of the presence of God and wanting in his disturbing way to seek God's will and come before God's face.

The last two pieces are from Elias's newsletters, and the subject-matter, like the letters to Cahal, tell us something more about his view of life.

Prologue July 1961

My dear Cahal,

I have often meant to write to you about the religious life because somehow or other your views seem to correspond to mine. You have never amounted to much in the religious life, nor have I; but there is a new wind in the religious life and the voices of little men begin to be heard. You know, we look back to the prophets and to the saints and they will tell us what to do. The great men, the big men, particularly those who put their thoughts down on paper, these we hear, these we read about, but we never hear what the little men have to say. We have heard the roarings of the lions, we have never heard the whimperings of the rabbits. Above all we have never heard the chitterings of the swallows, the little men whose thoughts fly above the level of other men, and go unrecorded because they are of no more account than the whisperings of the wind in the trees.

So often I have driven through the Kentish lanes and byroads and have listened to the soft winds of the poplars that provide a wind break to the hops. You see them around most of the hop-fields breaking the wind that should not shake the blossom and I have thought why it is that there is so little to break the wind on us.

126

4. **Fourth Disc**   1st August, 1961.

My dear Cahal,

Have you ever thought about the terrific contribution of the B.B.C.
to musical literature? I never listened to the B.B.C. very much until
now. I was always too busy. Now I lie in bed and listen to the eight
O'clock news and what follows. I never knew until lately that there
was a "d" in Mozart. Mind you, you can't see it, there is not a shred
of evidence that it ever existed. But it is there – official and I think
permanent. It is now Modzart. You live and learn!

When I was a boy I was terrified by the scowling bust of Beethoven.
To me he seemed like an old man who had swallowed a whole dishful of
crickets and that his chances of survival were small. I just could not
associate him with music. Now that I have grown up I know that the face
I once feared is the face of a thinker and that beauty is no part of God's
plan for mankind. It consoles me very much my dear Cahal, because I have
never been beautiful myself. The last time I saw you I didn't think that
you were very beautiful either, but I think you will come to the four
crossings where men say "Good-night" with a peaceful if not complacent
mind.

One time in Dublin I wanted to go to confession on a Saturday night.
I had my preferences like everyone else, and just as I went into the
confessional the priest stood up and went away. Having made such a public
exhibition of my intentions I ducked in next door to the very man that I
always disliked. I disliked him because of his face. I thought that he
was proud, imperious and insensitive, and that he had no time for little
people.

I had a problem on my mind – the big problem of my life, and do you
know my dear Cahal that he received me with such understanding and sympathy
that he resolved the whole matter for me. I was his last penitent that night—
that Saturday night of all Saturday nights that changed my life. I never
told him because I did not think for a moment that he would have remembered
anything about it.

My dear Cahal, all I have said to you now should make you very careful
of what you say in the confessional. What I have said should make you pray
for Grace to say the right word, to never let tiredness, boredom, or anything
else interfere with your advice to sinners. He never knew that the five
minutes he spent on me changed my life. I was always too shy to tell him.
He lived out his mortal span and I do not suppose that he once in his after
life ever realised that a few minutes in the confessional changed the life of
a boy for better, or for worse. When you go into the confessional never be
in a hurry and never say to yourself, "This is just another one." Never get
bored with the repetitions of little men, because one day into your world
may swim the big fish and only you can catch and save him. I was not a big
fish.

The transcript of Elias Lynch's letters to Cahal.

127

I intend to dictate a short letter each day from now on. I hope you won't find them too boring. I never suffered from a shortage of words, although occasionally from a shortage of ideas. When I was younger I did not write because I was not mature enough. Now that I am old I do not write because I am too tired. Maybe the underlying reason for such mental laziness is I never felt I had anything important to say. I have suffered from people who had nothing to say and would insist on saying it. If I begin to tire you, please stop me. I have often told you that you talk too much, but it is an Irish fault. We are, I think, the greatest conversationalists since the Greeks. We enjoy talking. We enjoy the cut and thrust of rapier-like conversation. Sometimes we can wound an adversary, but it is seldom unkind, the wounds easily heal. The Chinese love setting off fire crackers. So, too, we love to set the heather blazing in a fury of words. You and I are now old enough to know that words mean very little, but let us enjoy the sparkle of them, before our eyes grow too dim to see the answering glint in each others eyes. It is a good thing that I am dictating this on a recording machine because the disc keeps me within bounds, otherwise I might go on forever.

On being a Carmelite

My dear Cahal,

I have often heard you say that you could not, or would not, have ever been anything else but a Carmelite. I have said so myself. It is a gross exaggeration because we would neither of us have been Carmelites except by the will of God. Call it accident or design, but here we are after forty years service in the ranks. We have never amounted to very much, minor command in an unimportant set-up. Mind you I am not saying that it hasn't been very nice; I am not saying that I have not enjoyed it. You have I know, and you are a better mixer than I am. It took me a long time to find out that ordinary people regarded me as rough and tough, many of them had never had the time to find out that there was, and is, a kinder side to my nature. How many times have you stood before the world solid on your own two feet trying to look unshakable as the rock of Gibraltar, and how many times have you gone back to your room feeling just like a frightened fool.

Sometimes I get called to hear confessions. Mostly it is the ordinary confectionary stuff, but one must never neglect the confession bell because once in a while there swims in the big fish and then you feel that your profession is worth while. It is like a doctor. You are curing a cold, you are trying to do something for a cancer. That is why we are never off parade.

The trouble about letters like this is that when I get called away I do not remember what I have said before, nor have I the time or patience to review what I have already said in the light of what I may say again. As I have said to you before my dear Cahal I am bone lazy. I am not bone lazy because I am short of words, I am just tired of repeating them. I am glad that we do not belong to a great overpowering and magnificent religious order where the individual is crushed by the magnificence of his own organization and his only outlet is to talk about the Order to which he belongs. They parade the religious world like guardsmen. One always feels that behind them stands the all powerful organization. In the light of it they walk, they talk and confront the world.

You know Cahal, you and I can go forth into the world of men and tell them that we are Carmelites and there are few people who if you told them we belonged to the Camel Corps would hardly know the difference. Isn't it consoling to belong to a regiment of little men, the sons of the prophet, the heirs of the tradition of Mount Carmel where men lived in caves and called themselves hermits and were driven back into the world of men only by the sword of the Saracens. Sleep well, my friend, because you will not be murdered tonight.

Being sensitive when hearing confessions

My dear Cahal,

Have you ever thought about the terrific contribution of the B.B.C. to musical literature? I never listened to the B.B.C. very much until now. I have always been too busy. Now I lie in bed and listen to the eight o'clock news and what follows. I never knew

129

until lately that there was a "d" in Mozart. Mind you, you can't see it, there is not a shred of evidence that it ever existed. But it is there – official – and I think permanent. It is now Modzart. You live and learn!

When I was a boy I was terrified by the scowling bust of Beethoven. To me he seemed like an old man who had swallowed a whole dishful of crickets and that his chances of survival were small. I just could not associate him with music. Now that I have grown up I know that the face I once feared is the face of a thinker and that beauty is no part of God's plan for mankind. It consoles me very much my dear Cahal, because I have never been beautiful myself. The last time I saw you I didn't think you were very beautiful either, but I think you will come to the four crossings where men say "Goodnight" with a peaceful if not complacent mind.

One time in Dublin I wanted to go to confession on a Saturday night. I had my preference like everyone else, and just as I went into the confessional the priest stood up and went away. Having made such a public exhibition of my intentions I ducked in the next door to the very man I always disliked. I disliked him because of his face. I thought that he was proud, imperious and insensitive, and that he had no time for little people like me.

I had a problem on my mind – the big problem of my life – and do you know my dear Cahal that he received me with such understanding and sympathy that he resolved the whole matter for me. I was his last penitent that night, that Saturday night of all Saturday nights that changed my life. I never told him because I did not think for a moment that he would have remembered anything about it.

My dear Cahal, what I have said to you now should make you very careful of what you say in the confessional. What I have said should make you pray for Grace to say the right word, to never let tiredness, boredom, or anything else interfere with your advice to sinners. He never knew that the five minutes he spent on me changed my life. I was always too shy to tell him. He lived out his mortal span and I do not suppose that he once in his life ever realised that a few minutes in the confessional changed the life of a boy, for better or for worse. When you go into the confessional

130

never be in a hurry and never say to yourself, "This is just another one." Never get bored with the repetitions of little men, because one day into our world may swim the big fish and only you can catch and save him. I was not a big fish.

A parable about temptation

My dear Cahal,

I have some friends in Nice and years ago I was sitting on the promenade looking out at the sea. The famous Promenade des Anglais. I was thinking of the many famous people who had walked up and down since the days when King Eddie had made the place famous, and I was just wondering if any famous people were still around. Just down below me was the famous Hotel Ruhl where King Farouk used to hold court. It was too expensive for me to frequent that part of the sea front. Fashionable people don't like walking where there is not a crowd, and there was no crowd where I sat.

There I sat in a white panama hat, a light coat, smoking my pipe. Along came a gypsy girl, maybe she was twelve years old; I wouldn't know. She looked at me. She circled round. She leaned on the railings of the sea front and looked out at the waters. Then she turned and looked straight at me. It was a little disturbing. Into my mind came all the old thoughts of bygone years, when I listened to stories of the evil eye, telling your fortune, or your future. After a while I began to think that I had had enough of it. I searched in my pocket to find a one hundred franc piece, worth a shilling. I beckoned her and she took it. She stepped back a few paces. Then I saw her looking, as it were, over my head. I did not know that she was looking at my hat. I smiled at her – it is the only way to convert a girl into friendliness. She came over and pointed at my hat. I was very puzzled, so I took off my hat and looked at it. My hat was alright. When I looked at her again she stretched out her hand, took my panama, smiled gracefully and off she went, leaving me bald-headed on the Promenade des Anglais. My bald head is not an impressive sight anywhere but least of all upon the sea front at Nice. She walked away, slowly at first, and

131

then more quickly, and when she had gone fifty yards she looked back to see my puzzled face. Then she ran like a hare across the boulevard and down a side street.

I have often wondered since, my dear Cahal, what really happened to my panama hat. I had to buy another one the same evening. Where is my panama now? Is it worn by some old granddad of the gypsy tribe? Has it ever found its way to the Camargue?

My dear Cahal have you ever wanted to grab something so very badly, to take it, and run for your life? I often have. Most of us feel this temptation at one time or another in our priestly life to take what you want and run away. There is an old Portuguese proverb which runs, "God says, take what you want, <u>but pay for it.</u>" You and I are old enough to see how that truth works out. Have you ever had anything in your life that you didn't pay for? I certainly haven't. It is a thought that should go deeply down into our consciences.

A dose of realism

My dear Cahal,

It is nearly thirty years since I came to Faversham. I remember very well the day I walked up Stone Street and saw the twin towers ahead of me. I thought to myself, "This is it," but I was wrong. I found that I was looking at the chapel of the local Almshouses. I asked a man standing by, "Where is the Catholic Church around here?" He said, "You will find up there behind the wall." He was perfectly right. Behind the wall it was. The dingiest little box you ever saw. Then I knew what the Carmelites really did think of me! There was an old rambling presbytery. Five entrances to it on the ground floor and you never knew at any time of the day or night if you would find a traveller seeking your advice or prepared to give it to you.

The first Sunday's collection was seventeen and eight pence. At that time the Irish Province could not afford to send me more than half a crown daily Mass stipends. I began to wonder if I would have to get a job delivering newspapers. I walked round the town for six months and came to the conclusion that I could do it for the rest of my life and nothing would happen, except destitution.

The people came to Mass, but they didn't seem glad to see me. They didn't seem to want to talk to me. I could find no friendliness anywhere. It took me a long time to realize that they were just scared of me. I found that the Catholic Church stood lower than the Salvation Army. Shopkeepers would not deliver goods on credit; cash on delivery.

I tell you, my dear Cahal, it got me down. I found myself looking in the glass to find out any criminal tendencies in my face. In the end I decided that my nose was too big. It is still too big, I regret to say; but I have long since ceased to consider its magnitude. Since then I have made a study of many famous noses, "Schnozzzle" Durante included, and I have decided that noses do not matter.

In our novitiate we met that master of the religious life called Roderiguez. He told us stories to show how a religious should behave and followed it up by sledgehammer examples of neglect of the preceding doctrine. It was all taken from the Franciscan tales of the Annals of the Desert of the Nile; examples of what could happen if the brethren did not behave according to the rule.

I like men with big noses now. I never miss Ted Moult on B.B.C. television. When I see him I say to myself, "If he can go through life with a nose like that, why can't I?" He is a farmer and I am a priest, and cows are not critical.

You see, my friend Cahal, <u>how little things can get you down</u>. How a matter of noses can so distort your vision that your nose can become more important than the rest of you.

I was young then, so young that I hate to think of it. But I grew out of it. I made up my mind that I would stay in Faversham six months and no longer, and I have been here ever since, for nearly thirty years.

Last Sunday I consecrated a burial plot in the local cemetery and it provides the burial ground for six Carmelites as well. I have been around here so long that it is not worth my while to go home. In all that time it has been like digging a hole in the ground; the longer you dig, the deeper it gets, and the harder it is to climb out of it, until finally you accept your fate and invite the world to shovel the clay back on top of you when God wills that you should lie down.

My dear Cahal, you may think your destiny is in your own hand, but that is a tragic mistake. Your destiny is in the hands of God and in the hands of your Superiors, and there is little you can do about it.

One thing you can do is to pray to God for grace to do His will. To accept with fortitude and resignation the lot he has handed out to you. In that way you will carry the <u>cross that He has made for you</u> and what better lot would a Christian crave.

Sleep well, my friend.

Hermit tradition

My dear Cahal,

I have often wondered about the ancient Carmelites, the men who fled before the sword of the Saracens and came back to Europe with the returning Crusaders. Today we are inclined to think that the world is lost to Communism. It must have seemed to those men that the world was lost to the Saracens; that the Star and the Crescent have triumphed over the Cross for all times.

It was some time before 1240 when those battered hermits from the caves of Carmel found dry land on the Kentish shore. Not many were priests. Soldiers from the Crusades turned hermits. Pilgrims who fought their way to the Holy Land and did not want to come home. What is it that makes a man a hermit? Piety of course, and a strong desire to get away from it all. But Mount Carmel was not a fortress, nor was it a defence against the perils of war. There is an old saying "If your wife tells you to jump out of the window make sure you are on the ground floor." There should always be a way out. There was not much room for passengers in the returning ships of the Crusaders but a few did come home and between them and the Crusaders was forged a strong link, rather like the link that binds ex-servicemen today.

Nearly every vagrant that went from door to door after the Napoleonic Wars claimed that he had fought at Waterloo. It was

134

all the better if he had lost an arm, or an eye, or could show a wooden leg.

It has always been a miracle to me how those old hermits survived in the closely organized ecclesiastical network of the England of that time. I think their link with the Crusaders pulled them through. They were not accepted into what could be called desirable residential areas, they had to fend for themselves on the fringes of towns. It must have been a hard fight. Our Lady must have spread her mantle over those displaced hermits. That they grew into a religious order is one of the marvels of ecclesiastical history.

Seven hundred years have gone by, and you would think that the Carmelites have changed radically. They have not. One can still feel the old heremitical tradition. I have lived in Carmelite houses for short periods and one gets the impression that the men are isolated from each other by some invisible barrier. They seem to keep out of each other's way. Some Carmelites are intense individualists. The *Rule* says we must live together, think together and act together, but somehow it does not work out that way. Is it that we are destined in the end to go back to the old heremitical life, so that we may find liberty of the spirit and that individuality of purpose that we always seem to pursue? I do know. I am too old now to solve that problem. Certain it is that I could never live in any other mind of a religious order. We belong to the least regimented of all the orders in the Church.

A big dog and little men

My dear Cahal,

Tanners Street, where I live, is like Harry Lauder's stick, a compromise between a corkscrew and a hairpin bend. A dense ring of trees surround us and the birds twitter gaily when the weather is fine. If you are up very early in the morning you can see things that would startle you. A cock and hen pheasant picking on the lawn outside, squirrels searching for nuts in the hazel trees. No wonder we never see any. I planted them years ago so that we might have a few Kent cobs for Christmas, but

135

the squirrels always get there first. They are the red squirrels, not those grey tree rats we sometimes see. There are two pigeons who come as well, a rabbit now and again, and one morning I saw a hare sparring in the sunken garden. He was fighting nobody but himself. It made me think that curious behaviour is common to animals as well as to men.

Our shrubs have been there long enough now to look their best. The hydrangeas are a crown of blossom and the floribunda roses bloom from May to December. Altogether a delightful place to live in.

My office window looks upon the garden. I can see the printing house staff coming and going. I can hear the chatter of the girls talking to the dog. A huge Alsatian called Rex. He terrifies everybody. He is known locally as the Catholic dog. A very close relation of the devil; completely unreasonable, dangerous and to be avoided at all costs. In reality he is a big fraud. He falls flat upon his face in adoration if a woman comes round the corner. He knows he has a way with women. In fact he can get away with anything if only he acts his part. Isn't it peculiar, my dear Cahal, how big people get on well with women? How big dogs can make women their slaves? It is amazing to see travellers in the paper and printing machinery, arriving at the gate, ringing the bell and being escorted down past this fearsome animal who always looks as if it has already had a little man for breakfast.

My dear Cahal, you have always had a way with women. I think it is that chuckle in your voice. It is certainly not the beauty of your face. You will be surprised how nicely people speak of you behind your back. They think your merits have gone unrecognized for years; that you are, as a matter of fact, a big fish in a little pond whereas you ought to be a whale of a success. I don't know, my dear Cahal. It is good to find nice men in little places even if you talk too much. Somehow or other I like a fellow who talks too much. They are a great improvement on these awful characters one sometimes meets in religious life. Sometimes you meet them as subjects. Sometimes you meet them as Superiors and they are one and all alike. They are a one-man secret society. They go out. They come in. Where they have been they never say. What they have done they never mention. Usually they do not read and

136

therefore have not one idea to rattle against another inside their heads. It is hard to live with them.

My dear Cahal, let us pray that you and I for all the years that are left to us may never be condemned to live in a house where conversation is forbidden, but encouraged. God gave us speech so that we could bring joy to our neighbour. They kill whatever life there is. How surprising it is that they are all such honest fellows, such good religious, and invariably such inoffensive characters. Maybe God built them without guile.

Sleep well, my friend.

Awkward or ill!

My dear Cahal,

The ancient Greeks had an axiom – "Know thyself". I well remember in my younger years how I used to reproach myself on my lack of zeal in the service of God. The *Rule* exhorted us to rise with alacrity in the early hours and go gaily to choir to sing the Divine Praises, and to spend a half hour in meditation. These things I did from a sense of duty aided by the bell; but I did not have enough energy to swat a fly on a page of my breviary, let alone sing gaily. And flies there were. There was no end to the stick I invented to beat myself for my lack of service to the Lord. Whether it was the long walk to college or in devotion to the studious life, I always seemed to be lacking. Yet I wanted to be a priest, I wanted to serve God, and I wanted to do a number of other things as well, but I always seemed to be just one step behind. I was thrown out of choir because I sang too loudly. I was too awkward to belong to the graceful liturgical squads that served in the Roman functions. In fact, I hardly seemed to fit in anywhere – even on the bus. My legs were too long. The short Romans used to look at me as much as to say, "You ought to pay twice, because you take up twice as much room."

I never seemed to have enough energy to perform the daily tasks, but my head was always working. It went on and on. My desires outstripped my efforts.

137

After many years of parochial life I was concerned that my eyesight was failing. I went to see our doctor who told me after some inspection that I was a diabetic, that I would have to take things easy. <u>Good God</u>! I had been beating myself with a stick all my life to make myself go harder under the illusion that I was <u>just lazy</u>, and now I was told to take things easy and go slow. It has made a difference, but not much. My head still goes on and on. It keeps on turning and I have to turn with it. There is one consolation. Now I know the reason why I am lazy. Now I know the reason why I cannot run. Now I know why I could never be bothered to play golf or to dig the garden, and why it is I never had the ambition to out-walk a fellow up the hill and over the top. Now I know why it is I always just wanted to sit down and think.

It is a question of sugar, my dear Cahal, because sugar is converted into energy and without a balanced diet of carbohydrates, protein and fats, we are nothing more than a human cripple in a physical sense.

This is Friday, and our housekeeper gave me a breakfast composed of porridge and milk; toast and tea. She just doesn't understand that a man cannot live on a diet like that; that he requires protein and fats as well. She hasn't got enough intelligence to go out and buy a herring or a kipper for breakfast. I don't want to eat; I don't want to drink. In fact I have an abhorrence of all food. I just want to stay alive. You cannot love the stuff if you think that it is going to kill you unless you take a large dose of insulin. The large dose of insulin will kill you unless you take food. Anyway, God bless the man who discovered insulin, Dr. Frederick Grant Banting, 1891-1941; he has given me a few more years to live.

The Vicar of Wakefield and a word too many

My dear Cahal,

I have been thirty-one years in Faversham. It is a long time. I did not come here; I was sent - for my sins. I was eighteen months in Sittingbourne, which in the eyes of Faversham people is a third-class residential area, so that from that point of view it was a

138

relief. I used to go for an hour's walk in the twilight and a stroll among the orchards was the only real relief from the continual buzz and screech of the highway that flowed passed our door.

One of the reasons for my removal to Faversham – the emphasis is on the word "removal" – was the fact that I was featured in a Sunday newspaper. I took advice from a prominent layman who said the one thing Sittingbourne needed was a Catholic social centre, so I hired premises next door on a five years' lease. It was upstairs and was called "Whitefriars Hall". There was a bar, because that seems to be the only way of keeping people in a place after nine thirty at night. Everything went wrong, my dear friend. The caretaker put his head in the gas oven because he was unhappy with his wife, and everything seemed to pile up just as if there was a jinx on the place. To crown it all, a London journalist heard about this venture and billed me as "Mine host of Whitefriars Arms."

That as you know, my dear Cahal, is enough to wreck a very large battleship let alone a very small schooner like me. When the solemn conclave of Carmelite elders met in Dublin, they shook their heads and considered what should be done.

It was near the time of the Provincial Chapter and the result was that I was sent into exile at Faversham where I couldn't possibly do any further harm. They were right! It took me nearly two years to recover my equilibrium and a further Chapter passed into history. I was left where I was.

Today Faversham is the financial pivot of the Anglo-Welsh Carmelite Province. In fact, without Faversham the Anglo-Welsh province would never have existed, and couldn't exist even now, unless by some miraculous intervention of God.

Now, my dear Cahal, I want to point out something that may not be news to you. It is this: that sometimes when catastrophe overwhelms us, when we know we have sunk to the bottom, it is only the beginning of a rise to the top. I rose to nothing during my life.

My brethren found that I had a certain flair for raising money and they left me at it for thirty years. I will die in harness.

When I tell these things to you I am omitting to describe the scars that these happenings made in my pride and self-respect.

139

When I came to Faversham I felt I was the least of all my brethren. When I saw the house in which I was to live, I was confirmed in my impression; and when in saw the church, I said to myself, "I wish they had sent me to Africa." However, this is not a story about Faversham, but about Sittingbourne.

It is over forty years ago since I first read "The Vicar of Wakefield" and I was so impressed with the opening paragraph of it that I memorized it. It has remained indelibly printed on my mind ever since as the perfect picture of a parson and a parson's wife. It was written by Oliver Goldsmith at a time when Protestantism was settling down into respectability, when it had lost its revolutionary fervour and felt secure. In other words, it was the Bolshevists turned into a Bourgeoisie. "The Vicar of Wakefield" is one of the minor classics of the English language and I think that as long as the language endures it will be read and enjoyed because it is one of the most perfect pictures of an age that has ever been written. Here is the passage I refer to, the opening chapter of the "Vicar of Wakefield".

"I was ever of the opinion, that the honest man who married and brought up a large family did more service than he who continued single and only talked of population. From this motive, I had scarce taken orders a year before I began to think seriously of matrimony, and chose my wife, as she did her wedding gown, not for a fine glossy surface, but such qualities as would wear well. To do her justice, she was a good natured, notable woman; and as for breeding, there were few country ladies who could show more. She could read any English book without much spelling; but for pickling, preserving, and cookery, none could excel her. She prided herself also upon being an excellent contriver in housekeeping; though I could never find that we grew richer with all her contrivances."

That passage has remained in my memory for forty years. I still think that it is a picture of a scene that may endure forever, in spite of changes in times. I can never meet a parson, or a parson's wife, without trying to see in him and her the Vicar of Wakefield and his devoted spouse. I think that it is only the Irish humour of Oliver Goldsmith that could have lightened up so that the pages of "The Vicar of Wakefield" remain like an illuminated manuscript as a picture of his time.

One day I went up to the local Cottage Hospital in Sittingbourne. I saw the people I needed to see, and then I met the Matron for the first time. A tall, good looking woman, very graceful, with a beautiful voice. It was half past twelve and she charmed my heart by asking if I would like a glass of sherry. I said, "Yes." As I sipped it, my arm leaning on the mantelpiece, I saw a picture of a young parson and looking at it I declaimed to her the first paragraph of "The Vicar of Wakefield". She listened with great interest and then said to me "That is my fiancé." She looked the most unparsonic wife I have ever seen, but I am certain that she was an enormous success.

I walked home, a journey of some twenty minutes, and from the time I stepped from the doorway until I reached my own, I kept repeating to myself, "Why don't you learn to keep your big mouth shut."

I have often said the same thing since. I have never learned to keep my big mouth shut, neither have you. Maybe that is why I like you; because in my late years it has been my misfortune to live with young assistants, young priors, or whatever else you can call them who conduct their lives and business in complete isolation. They behave as if they were a one-man secret society. That imposes a hard penance on an old-timer in a parish. I have lived in Faversham thirty-one years. I may live just a few more years, I am not very hopeful that I will live much longer. Do you know my dear Cahal, that people may die and be buried, children can be born and baptized, that people can be married and go on their way without any mention whatever of the fact to the community. It is hard sometimes when one sees a child that one has baptized, either marrying, or dying and being buried, and no mention made of it at table or in casual conversation.

Keep your big mouth shut! God forgive me, but let me have the man who was born with his mouth wide open instead of having a button hole in the front of his face. Keep these things in mind, my dear Cahal. You are too old to benefit by them now and I am on my way out, but maybe someone will read these lines in days to come and learn that keeping your big mouth shut is not the

141

whole secret of life. There are times and even occasions, when one should keep it open; to a wide degree.

Not an easy vocation

What a thought it is! How a casual encounter in the porch of a church can start a reaction that will change the lives of three men, who in struggle and strife will one day arrive at the priesthood.

In the years that followed I often had doubt s about my vocation. I met enormous difficulties and I had not an easy temperament to meet them, but I said to myself, "God is merciful and forgiving and surely He means me to persevere; or He would never have let me in for what I have had to endure in these years that followed His call.

I never became important in the Order. I was too independent, too blunt, and dreadfully negligent of the feelings of others; but I found a niche that suited my peculiar mentality. I developed a flair for raising money and have now been doing it for over twenty years. I have devoted my life to raising money for our seminaries and for the support of students, and to the propaganda necessary to achieve it. I have often wondered if that is enough to gain the Kingdom of Heaven.

As a professed student of the Carmelites I came to know many classical superiors. They were right in feeling great contempt for our scholastic achievements. They were not quite right in assessing our intellectual potentialities. As students of the National University we used either to walk or to cycle to lectures in the mornings and then to lunch at Whitefriars, within the city, at a table so low that our voices couldn't be heard. Occasionally after lunch we were waylaid by these classical scholars. A favourite trick of Father Thomas Kelly, the bearded Greek expert, was to invent a quotation and to ask us where it came from. He would first ask what Shakespearean play we were studying at the University and then he would trot out a quotation, and of course if you were foolish enough to say you knew where it came from, he looked at you as much as to say, "You are just what I thought." He had made it up himself.

My dear Cahal, there can be no generation of men so cruel, so uncompromising and even so unhelpful, as the classical scholar who feels his position is so insecure that his word is almost law. Thank God, my dear Cahal, that neither you nor I have ever figured as classical scholars.

There is much upon which you and I can pride ourselves. All these men are dead. Their learning and their knowledge faded with them into the grave. Snobs of education, they have not left a word behind them that can be remembered. They are as if they never lived. Some men live by their teachings; some men by their writings; some by their discoveries, and some live by their work. That is why, my dear Cahal, being a late vocation myself, I want to be remembered even in a little way by the work I have done. I am not a great writer. I cannot write English prose that men may remember. I am just writing to you, but there is something I need to say. I want to recall the miseries, the fears, the useless efforts that I had to make even to surface for recognition as an educated man. Even now I sometimes wonder about it. I do know that I have worked hard, that I have never thought about anything else but the Carmelite Order. If you have struggled hard and emerged, the memory of it will never leave you. I say this to you, my dear Cahal, so that I may encourage young men, in bowler hats and belted raincoats, to attempt the impossible. Maybe not to the priesthood but to the lay brothership of the Carmelite Order. The struggle did certainly wear me to the bone, but men can be brave when God leads them in. I have never sought to be amongst the first or the last in the kingdom of God. All I have sought is to be among the multitude who – signed with the cross in the waters of baptism – seek sanctuary with God by the merits of the blood of Christ.

Longing to be a hermit

My dear Cahal,

We are both old Irish Carmelites, and as usual with Carmelites our history is handed down by word of mouth and not in written records. How we would love to have some of the writings of old

143

father Sprat, just to show what kind of a man he was; what he thought about; how he lived and what he hoped to do. At the end of this letter I will give a few facts about that extraordinary man, if I can find records of it.

That is why I am writing to you my dear Cahal. In a hundred years time you and I will be dead, and not remembered, if we do not leave behind us something, however imperfectly expressed, as a memory of the Carmelites of our time, the young people who will be Carmelites of the future will have nothing to pin down and say, "This is what a Carmelite of 1961 thought and did."

We are part of history whether we like it or not. Let us be at least vocal even if we are dead. Some of the Carmelites of today are great men. Will they ever stay on record as having done anything at all?

We are the successors of the old heremitical tradition. We are not men of records. We are not dedicated to libraries or museums. In fact I think we are, by the very fact that we are Carmelites, dedicated to oblivion. I do not mean by that that we are dedicated to die. I do not think that ever the day will come when there will not be a Carmelite Order. I think that we have in our tradition more promise of survival than any other religious order or congregation that I know. If I were a young man again, and if I felt I had a religious vocation, there is no order or congregation in the whole earth to which I would give my allegiance except the Carmelites. We are the least regimented of all. We are not ordered about, and there is great scope for individual expression. In fact, I think that we are an order of individualists.

I know that in the course of the centuries they have tried to turn us into another pattern. One General Chapter, one General after another, has tried to make us conform to a pre-accepted plan; but somehow we have always resisted it. There is behind every man who wears the Carmelite habit the desire to be rid of it all and go back to the desert, or to the mountains, rather than to be pushed around.

I feel that now myself. I feel the call of the desert and of the mountains. In fact I would just like to walk out into the desert sand and call it a day. I spent several months lying in a hospital bed, racked by pain and rolled about by nurses. They were not

144

unfeeling, they were just doing their job. They were rough but nice. I still remember them; and I wonder to myself that some men desire a long time before dying. Do we not, my dear Cahal, at our time of life live both day and night in the presence of God, is not our life a ceaseless meditation?

Let us go when His Holy Will decides.

The English and moderation

My dear Cahal,

The Englishman's behaviour in a railway carriage is taken as typical of him outside it. If he is not reading the paper he wraps himself up in impenetrable silence. He may look at the scenery, or he may quietly review your shoelaces, but it is quite probable that he may leave the carriage without knowing if you had a moustache or not. He rigidly preserves the reputation of being a man who minds his own business and is not concerned with yours. Ask him a question, and he will answer it courteously, but briefly, and armed with rolled umbrella and bowler hat to go on his way to the City. The unflappable man!

He doesn't talk; except in a pub. But then the pub is a sort of club for him and his friends. He is a man of grave aspect given to the art of understatement. You could count upon the fingers of both hands the number of adjectives he uses in normal conversation – unless he is a politician. There is a grave danger that we will run short of adjectives suitable to politicians, particularly of the Opposition. They have already exhausted the dictionary. I started making a list of adjectival rockets fired at the Government from Labour benches, but I gave it up. I was afraid that I might spoil my own style of speech.

It is that gift of understatement which makes the word of an Englishman, whether spoken or written, so powerful in the world. It grew up in the days of Queen Victoria and has since been sanctified by tradition. When, in the days of Victoria, a note went to some foreign potentate or nation that "Her Majesty's Government is gravely concerned" it was usually a preparatory gesture before delivering an almighty kick in the pants. These

145

notes never went as far as to say, "Her Majesty's Government is upset." Oh, no, Her Majesty's Government is never more than gravely concerned.

The result of this is that when an Englishman says something, or writes something, the world is inclined to believe him. People think that it is a great trouble to him to say anything at all, and that what he does say is so moderate in tone that it is the gospel truth. That is how English propaganda during the War persuaded thousands of people that Hitler really did chew carpets.

There is a lesson for us in this, particularly for us who are called upon to preach the word of God – to avoid exaggeration, to shun the resounding adjective – to preach the word of God coolly, calmly and without hysteria. Religion is a normal thing in life; it does not need to be buttressed by a formal array of superlatives, and the fiery preacher usually finds out in the end that he has been merely beating the air. Saint Paul says we mustn't do that. Fire-eating Saint Paul. The fiery zealot amongst the apostles turns out to be almost factual in his use of words. He uses non-threats. He talks as a plain man to plain men. He points out the snares that beset men's paths, but he is far more moderate a preacher than many of the famous preachers I have read in the past. And yet he can send a shiver up your spine as readily as the best. As a preacher, and a teacher, he is supreme amongst all.

Ready to be compassionate

My dear Cahal,

Shortly after Brother Anthony and I moved down here I was having a cup of tea one Sunday morning after late Mass. I was relaxed and felt that I had preached a good sermon. It was on charity, the love of one's neighbour.

The front door was open and the next thing I knew was that a rather good-looking young lady stood before me, dressed in an expensive fur coat with the rest to match. If you want to know if a lady is really smart look at her shoes. They were perfect! I knew her, but not well. She introduced herself. Her husband, whom we have never seen, was in the Merchant Navy; a good man you understand. There was a little daughter, the image of her mother. A terrible tragedy had come upon them. The remittance usually sent by her husband had not arrived on Friday; they had waited all day Saturday, and now it was Sunday and there was no food in the house. There were tears in her eyes. I was faced with the appalling prospect of a father, mother, married daughter and child going hungry on the Sabbath day. You will admit, my dear Cahal, that that is something no priest can tolerate. I thought first that we might give our own small shoulder of mutton and I wondered if we could have some tinned food ourselves; but she solved the matter for me by saying that a small matter of £5 would make it all right. I wondered where she would get anything to eat on a Sunday even if she had £5, but you remember, my dear Cahal, that these people have ways and means of doing things that are quite unknown to us. She got it! She thanked me and kept my hand in lingering thankfulness for quite a while. I can tell you, my dear Cahal, I felt noble and good.

After lunch I took my stick (in those days I used to walk) and sauntered down our street for my weekly survey of nature. I'm a great lover of nature as you know because I was born in the Wicklow Hills. I loved to go down to a place called Stonebridge Pond, wander through the paths and little bridges over waterways to watch the eels come wriggling upstream, and I loved to sit quiet and listen to the whirring of the wild ducks' wings as they flew in from the coast. I never ceased to admire the way they used to hit the water breast on, braking their impact with their webbed feet. I often wondered why it was that God had not given us a means of locomotion as swift as a wild duck, but then I realized that men live longer and go further, and God has to keep them in bounds by giving them two big feet. It would indeed be a tragedy, my dear Cahal, if we were all equipped like ducks.

Having decided on my Sunday afternoon's stroll, I sauntered down the street swinging my Irish black chasin as gallantly as I could. I passed the house of my friend in the fur coat. There was a furniture van outside the door and furniture was being removed. The van was half full. To show how innocent I was in those days my dear Cahal, no evil crossed my mind. I went on. I watched the eels and the ducks for a while and then came home through

147

the street of memories. The neighbouring women were standing at their front doors with their hands on their hips. I noticed there were no curtains on the windows of the house I was interested in. I asked a neighbour. She said, "They have moved to London, and good riddance." I had no answer to that after preaching a sermon on charity, but I knew I would never see that fur coat again and that I would never see my £5, and my self-confidence dropped to zero.

I never did see that fur coat again, but I heard that she was doing very well indeed in public relations in the West End of London.

My dear Cahal, what armour is one to wear against the world that comes against one in fur coats? Don't tell me that knowledge of the world is the safeguard. Many shrewder, cleverer and more experienced men than we are have fallen before pleading eyes and a soft voice and a touch of a lingering hand. I have often reflected on it and I have come to the conclusion that there is only one safeguard and that is prayer. Maybe John Henry Newman had words for it, "O Lord, support us all the day long of this troublesome life until the shades lengthen and the busy world is hushed, the fever of life is over, and our work is done. Then Lord in thy great mercy, grant us safe lodging, a holy rest and peace at last through Christ our Lord."

A balanced asceticism

My dear Cahal,

Some rethinking will have to be done in the future about this matter of fasting and abstinence. The old ideas that too much red meat put too much vitality into a man and thereby increased his sexual aberration is all wrong. It is like the old farming axiom "Don't give a horse too much oats or he will kick his heels." The trouble today is to get a horse to take oats; maybe he prefers mash, maybe he won't have oats at all.

I used to give retreats to nuns and found that certain nuns used to leave a little bit of sweet, or meat, upon their plates as an act of self denial. They didn't like to seem greedy. I wonder has it ever happened in the history of female conventual life that a nun sent up her plate to the Reverend Mother for a second helping? God be with me, but I wish I could see the day.

You see, my dear Cahal, the time has come when it is not a problem of people eating too much, but of people eating too little in the religious life. In spite of that we find religious superiors, both men and women, who try to pinch a penny off the cost of the table and yet demand from their subjects a penalty of service that would shock any trade unionist. You and I have some experience of mean pinching superiors, of men and women who thought they were serving God by not giving a decent meal to their subjects. There is a very special hell for these people but I will not condemn them to it.

There is a special danger in this matter, my dear Cahal, because if you find an inexperienced man or woman in charge of bringing up the younger generation, that they will try to preach, and even impose, self sacrifice at the table, and in the end reap for themselves and their community or congregation a generation of neurotics. A generation of young people who have been badly fed, badly reared, unevenly taught, and without that proper physical structure behind them that would enable them to think straight. All this is a mater of bad, wrongly directed ascetical instruction. The pink-faced novice who leaves something on his or her plate, under the idea that they are sacrificing something to God are not denying God, they are denying themselves the power to serve God. I have met nuns who told me they never touch sweets. Why? Because sweets are nice. Look at their starved, emaciated faces and don't jump to wrong conclusions. Just say to yourself, "Here is a woman who needs more sugar", whether that sugar comes from starch or otherwise, because that is what the woman needs. In other words, she needs feeding. Not starvation. Not self-sacrifice. She needs energy to lead a life in the service of God and mankind. Maybe she is a teaching or a nursing sister, probably a teaching sister because nursing sisters have got more common sense. Maybe they have more dietetic knowledge. The teaching and nursing professions need strong women, properly fed, devoid of aberrations which come from a lack of nutrition. You may not

149

know it, my dear Cahal, but it often means a lack of sugar, and lack of sugar means a lack of energy.

Try to keep this in mind because it may save our devoted sisters in religious congregations, teaching and otherwise, from being consigned to sanatoria because the religious life has denied them a properly balanced diet, by ill-informed superiors.

I am often asked by nuns to send them postulants. I often do. But I always make sure that there is no nonsense practiced at the community table by skinflint superiors, and I always find out if some privacy is given to hardworking men and women, and that they are not compelled to sleep in dormitories where no privacy is possible.

Do we have second sight?

My dear Cahal,

I came to Faversham thirty years ago and the town was just a little smaller than it is now. At night it was as quiet as an Irish village and even today you could almost shoot cats on the main street at ten o'clock at night without danger to the public.

It was a small mission. I was the only priest and I had a lay brother to look after me. I still look back on those years and wonder how it is we lived through them. I had very long legs, quite unsuitable to a bicycle, so I walked most places. I loved to go through the quiet lanes and back roads, through the orchards and hop fields, to see the life of the countryside. I would rather hear a cock crowing on a dunghill than the whistle of a railway train.

It was my duty to visit the local infirmary once a week. It was sited outside the town near an old brickfield. If you did not smell the infirmary upon your right you could smell the brickfield on your left. A quiet wall led up to it from the town called Lower road. There was a row of poor brick cottages leading off to the left; they were built on a bank and were high and dry even in wet weather. The brick makers lived there.

One seldom met anyone on the road to the infirmary, but people knew who I was because I wore a wide sombrero and carried a stick. There was a little bridge on the road and I used to look over the parapet to see if the eels had come up from the watercress beds. They used to lie in the shadow of the bridge away from the evening sun. There was a footpath and a tar and pitch wooden fence with a tangle of thorns behind it. It was a quiet road and I liked it.

There was a little girl I used to meet, maybe around eight years of age, certainly not ten. She was poorly dressed and I remember that her hair was tied with some sort of ribbon at the back. This left her face clear of shade and she had a long thin oval face with the loneliest eyes I have ever seen. She always wore half a smile. She was poorly dressed and her little socks hung down around her ankles and her shoes were worn. But the principle thing I noticed about her was her skipping rope. It had two wooden handles. I remember them well because they were red and blue handles and the paint was beginning to peel off. Sometimes she would be skipping, not very well, just amusing herself. Sometimes she would be holding her skipping rope in her hands and hopping about as I drew level with her and then she would watch me go by with a sort of intense curiosity. I was afraid to speak to her because I thought she was frightened of me, and might run away. Catholic children are never frightened of the priest, they like to notice the priest and be noticed by him. But she was not a Catholic.

She was nearly always there when I went up that road, always alone, always with her skipping rope. Then I used to just look at her, say "Hello", and pass on. I did this for a long time. She never answered me. It was queer in a way but I concluded that she was deaf and dumb. I wondered what her people were and why she had no companions. This went on for a long time and one day I said to myself, "I must find some clothes for that little girl." Then a thought came into my mind that stopped me in the road way. I said to myself, "I have known that little girl for four years, she has never got any bigger; she has always dressed in the same clothes and she is always handling the same skipping rope. How on earth does it happen?" I thought it very queer. Then I said to myself, "Maybe she has stopped growing because of some childhood ailment. Maybe she is deaf and dumb. Maybe her parents are working out in the fields. Maybe she has no friends because she doesn't want them."

151

I never tried to speak to her beyond saying "Hello" because I was afraid that I might frighten her. I spoke to a woman from Wallers Row one day and asked her if she knew the little girl down the road with a skipping rope. "Has she any parents – she doesn't seem to have any friends." The woman didn't know of any little girl down the road with a skipping rope. I said to her, "Maybe she can't talk. Is there a dumb child around Wallers Row?" "No", she didn't know of any.

Some time later on I came by some children's clothing, just the size for her. I made a parcel of them and the next time I went up that road I brought the parcel with me. Right enough, she was there with her skipping rope. I said, "Hello", and held out the parcel to her. All she did was to look at me with that silent stare. She didn't speak a word, she made no move to take the parcel, and feeling rather foolish I put it back under my arm and brought it home again.

Then they began building some bungalows in Lower Road and one day I met a young married woman coming out from one of them and I said to her, "Do you know the little girl up the road who plays with a skipping rope?" No, she didn't know any little girl with a skipping rope. By this time I was beginning to think that my lonely life was having an effect on my imagination. The lay brother who looked after me was deaf and I was very much turned inwards on myself.

One day I saw her again and I said "Hello", and walking ahead for some thirty yards I turned back and she was no longer in the road. Then I got the idea that she was a ghost and I started praying for her at Mass in the morning. It went on and on. I thought she grew more friendly and less afraid of me and one day I made up my mind that I would give her absolution. I knew that it was theologically improper to do it because you cannot absolve ghosts. Or can you? The words of the absolution *in quantum possum et tu indiges*, "as far as I can go according to your need." Next time I saw her, when I came to within thirty yards of her, I recited the conditional form of absolution and went through it right to the end as I drew level with her. I said "Hello" and passed on. Then I heard the dreadful screeching of the brakes of a lorry. I heard some cries and voices and the sound of bricks falling from the lorry on to the road and I found myself hanging on to the black fence in a state of mental confusion. I could smell the dust of falling bricks and I looked at the roadway and it was empty.

I never saw her again and to this day I do not know whether it was an actual experience or a dream.

Carry a Stick

The ways of the city have changed the ways of men. It is the city that sets the fashion. The bowler hat and the umbrella have returned to be the outward and visible sign of the high Civil Servant, the Banker, the Guard's Officer and the business man, but how few men do we see carrying a stick.

"Carrying a stick" is a peculiar expression. Men don't carry sticks, they use sticks, and it is not merely a custom, it is, in one sense, a necessity.

The stick has been man's companion long before he was adopted by the dog, and it was not that he carried a stick to keep the dog away. The stick has been the staff of the shepherd, the pilgrim and the mountain climber since the dawn of history. The Greek shepherd carried his crook, and the shepherd's crook became the pastoral staff of the Catholic bishop. That is why the crown of the pastoral staff curls in such a way. The ancient shepherd used his crook to catch the leg of the lamb or the sheep. He used a different sort of crook for each purpose. The crook became the symbol of the shepherd and is still the symbol of the bishop.

The only Greek bishop who gets into the news these days is Archbishop Makarios. If you see a photograph of him in the paper you will see that he carries a black ebony walking stick with a round silver top. The stick is long and he grasps it a little way down the shaft. That is how a pastor of souls displays his pastoral office.

The pastoral staff is often handed down from one Greek bishop to another, just as happens sometimes amongst Catholic bishops.

The famous Bantu cattle-herders in Africa carry long poles, blackened with age and smoothed by the constant grip of the

153

palm. Their sticks are so inseparable from them that they stand on their left leg, wind their right leg around the stick and go to sleep standing up. I have seen almost the same thing happen, but in a different way, to some ladies who use their shooting sticks at the races.

When I was in Wales I noticed that the sergeants in the Welsh police nearly all carry walking sticks, but the constables never. I wonder why? The Welsh farmers all carry sticks and it is very interesting to watch them at the cattle sales, how they guide the cattle into the stalls with a light touch of the stick on the jaw of the animal. They never ill treat animals with their sticks, but touch them lightly, and almost lovingly, to send them where they should go.

Every nation has its own type of stick. I remember when I was in Spain I carried with me an Irish blackthorn. It created tremendous interest. People came up to me and asked if they could have a look at it, and they go to great pains to explain that they, too, use walking sticks, but they are Malacca canes. The Malacca cane is much lighter than the Irish blackthorn.

In Ireland there is an expression, "Cut your stick and go." That was a literal truth. A man cut hi stick from the hedgerow before he started a journey. He trimmed it and it became his companion.

I knew a man who inherited a small acreage of bad land, and he didn't know what to do with it. I suggested to him that he should try to rear blackthorns and ash plants. He did, and he has now developed an export trade in dollars and is making a good living. He sometimes encloses the root of the blackthorn in a tin in order to shape it, because the best blackthorn finishes in a knob and not in a crook.

By planting the thorn trees and the ash with equal spacing six inches apart, the plants grow tall quickly. After the first two years the sproutings nearest the ground are nipped off, and so on each year until the sapling is tall enough to be cut. The crop is rotated so that a certain section comes to maturity each year. Plants that are slightly crooked can be straightened by steeping in water and then enclosing in a vice. Sometimes they are hung on the roof to dry and finally they are polished and varnished to suit the taste of the customer. The crook of the ash plant is turned in much the same way. First, the wood is softened by steaming, then it is turned gradually in a vice, and finally tied so that it can set.

The stick was a prime necessity of dress to the Georgian swell. It was nearly always a stick with either a gold or silver knob. The Georgian swell used it as a sort of pacing stick, and to be without his cane was most embarrassing because he didn't know what to do with his hands.

Have you ever thought about it? It is difficult to know what to do with your hands, and it is necessary to give your hands something to do. You can carry a pair of gloves, and that is something. Or, you can carry a brief case, and that can be a solution, but best of all is to carry a stick. Look at the things you can do with a stick. You can swing it, you can swagger with it, you can lean on it, you can tap your legs with it and you can swipe off the heads of the daisies as you go past. Without a stick a young man has to fall back on a packet of cigarettes. Stop a young man on the street. If he has a stick he is a happy man, if he has no stick he will immediately fish in his pocket for a packet of cigarettes in order to give his hands something to do.

This is the time of the year to cut a stick; when the sap is down. Maybe some countryman who reads this will take the trouble to cut me one and send it over. Trim it roughly, wrap a piece of rough sacking round it to protect the bark, tie a stout label on it and send it by post. One or more blackthorns or ash. We get many pilgrims here to the Shrine of Saint Jude, and many of them need a stick. I will put a metal tag on the sticks with a record of the Shrine of Saint Jude. Off you go.

Spiritualism

I met the devil only once, and that was not by appointment. This is the story. Take it or leave it.

I was stationed in a parish thirty years ago and one day I met a lady engaged in social work, and a point of religion came up which I explained as well as I could in casual conversation, and forthwith forgot about it. Weeks later I had a letter from her on another angle of the same problem, and I replied at length. It is a

155

hopeless job trying to explain theological questions on two pages of note paper. After some more exchanges I agreed to meet her. She could not come to me, I had to go to her, and it ended up with her asking for further instruction on Catholic belief.

That, of course, is a vague assignment. Anyway, I went to her cottage for six months twice a week, at some personal discomfort to myself. You see I was a young priest full of zeal anxious to convert the whole world. I did my best, but as time went on I began to feel that we were just talking. I decided to bring matters to a head. I said to her, "I have told you enough about the Catholic faith and now you must make up your mind. Do you want to be a Catholic or not?" She said, "No." "Well there you are," I said. She replied, "I just like to listen to you talking." I was so flabbergasted that I just could not trust myself to speak. I said to myself, "This woman has kept me talking for six months for nothing just because she liked to hear me talk." There is only one practical thing to do and that is to keep your mouth shut and go home. That I did! Diplomatic relations were at an end.

Months later I received a letter from her asking me about spiritualism. My thought was that I couldn't go on spending my life answering letters to people who are just curious. My reply was short. She had been dealing with spiritualists, mediums, table-writing, and so forth, and she was beginning to feel the effect of it on her mind. My reply simply said that if she didn't stop, she would either commit suicide or end up in a psychopathic ward. She was the daughter of a doctor. He was dead and she was the sole owner of a private mental home.

I didn't remember this until my letter had gone and when I did remember I said to myself, "That is the finish of it." Private mental homes thirty or forty years ago were simply camouflaged prisons for feeble-minded people. The minimum furniture, low quality food, locked doors, and the only relief a bell. If the bell rang too often it was simply cut off.

One evening I got a message asking me to come immediately. I knew what it was. At that time I had the feeblest of all cars, a vintage Morris Cowley. I set out on a late autumn evening and arrived at her home around 7p.m. She was a professional woman living with a woman who had a London practice and who, to my knowledge, was just as queer as she was. The country cottage divided in two, with the usual amenities, was approached by a public path through two fields divided by a stile. There was also a lane approach but I decided not to risk that because my lights were not too good and it would not be easy to turn around.

So I walked through the fields. I knocked and got no answer. The door was open and I walked in. Her bedroom was second on the left and it was in complete darkness. I found the light and then I saw something that completely astonished me. She was in bed with her arms outside the covers and she looked a picture of death. I sat beside the bed and tried to figure out what had happened.

Here we must go back on history. She had been deeply in love with an officer called Jack in the First World War. He died in the Battle of the Somme – the worst holocaust that has ever occurred in the history of England. Forty thousand men died in twenty minutes in an attack on the German entrenched positions. He was one of them. She was dedicated to him and it seemed to me that her whole desire in life was to find him again. Not in this life but in the hereafter. She sought the help of spiritualists, of mediums, of fortune tellers – in fact she tried to find out the eternal mysteries of God and of the hereafter so that she might be united with her lost lover. A very understandable position, but it led her into the land of the spirits and eventually into the land of the devil.

She had been to many spiritualistic meetings. She had asked these charlatans to bring before her the image of her dead lover, his voice, his personality. It was always the same story. It went something like this. Darling, I am unhappy, and never will be happy without you. Our souls are united, and our unity of soul is broken by the earth between us. I will be eternally unhappy, darling, until you can join me.

That was the message that continually cropped up. It cost her much money and great trouble of mind. In the end she bought a Ouija board. It is a board on which one can write on paper or otherwise, but the process is to empty one's mind completely and give over the mind and the will to the control of something else, maybe of the subconscious, maybe of some outside influence. Having bought this board she started to practice this emptying of

157

the mind and will and of submission to outside influence to guide her in her search. In the middle of the night she used to submit her emptied mind and will to the control of this influence and always the message was the same. "Darling I cannot live without you." There was only one conclusion to that plea and it stood out a mile – suicide.

One night she decided this was the only way out. She had been through a session with this devilish writing board and she decided the only thing to do was to end it all. It came to her after endless scribblings on paper, all of which lay beside the bed, haphazard and sometimes illegible.

She didn't know how to commit suicide but she found in the bathroom an open razor and she decided to cut her throat or her wrists. She was an Anglican and consequently had some residue of religion. She said, "If I am going to die I had better pray to God." She knelt down beside the bed and repeated the "Our Father" and suddenly the control broke, and she was free. She collapsed on the floor and was found there the following morning. She looked like a dead body in from the sea. Then she remembered my letter – "Either you will commit suicide or end up in a psychopathic ward" – and she decided to ring me.

I knew the story of Jack. I knew what she had been up to. I remembered my letter. She indicated by a motion of her hand that I should read the papers.

I have seen blasphemy. I have read obscenity, but I have never in my life imagined that a human being could be so immersed in blasphemy, in filth, in sex, and in hatred of God as was contained in those writings. I didn't read them all, they were too terrible. I lit a fire in the grate and burned the lot. Those writings frightened me because they were the writings of a human dominated by the spirit of evil, dominated by hatred of God and by the spirit of blasphemy. Having done that I looked at the burning papers and it seemed to me that the devil might jump out of the fireplace, but he didn't.

I said to myself, "What on earth can I do now? She is not a Catholic, what can I do?" I found water and salt and I blessed some holy water. I found in my pocket the unattached cross of a rosary beads, and a medal of Our Lady. I found a small safety pin on the dressing table and I pinned these on her breast. I blessed the room and I blessed her with holy water, then I made her repeat some prayers. Then I sat down to consider what I should do next. I could do nothing. She was asleep. I went quietly out. It was a fine moonlit night, and I started my way down the path through the fields.

About halfway down I knew there was something behind me. I could hear no footsteps, so I said to myself, "You are imagining things." In the end the feeling became so strong that I stopped and turned around to face my back tracks, and there I froze stiff. It was as if I could turn into a pillar of ice. I could see the cold sweat on the palms of my hands; I could feel it running down my chin and the back of my neck. My mind was paralysed and it seemed that I was pin-pointed on a precipice of terrible destruction. I could see nothing. I could feel nothing but the presence of a terrible evil, of malignity and hatred of God. I carried a stick in my hand and I crossed upon the path the sign of the cross. One thinks at such a moment of prayer. I didn't because I couldn't. I had only the strength to make the sign of the cross with the ferrule of my stick, and the only thing I could say was, "Don't come any further because if you do you are fighting the Cross of Christ." Maybe that was a prayer.

It was full moonlight and I saw nothing. I could only feel. I don't know how long I stood there, but I know things came to a deadlock. Eventually I turned and I reached the stile that divided the two fields. It was a simple practical English stile – one step up, wind your leg over the cross bar and one step down the other side. I remember sitting on the cross bar and looking at the track behind me, and saying to whatever it was, "Don't come past here."

Then there came to my mind the memory of the baptismal service where the child is anointed with the sign of the Cross and the devil is forbidden ever to violate it. I don't know how long I sat there but eventually I wound my other leg over the cross bar and went down the short field to the road. Half way down I said to myself, "I am safe now, I should make a run for it." But I didn't. Some streak of obstinacy in my nature said, "Take your time." Did I have at that moment the strength to hurry? I don't know. It was what I wanted to do. I came to the road and to the old car. I sat in it for a long time. My hands trembled but the cold was gone and my worst fears were over. I couldn't trust myself to turn the car round although the road was wide enough, so I drove a half mile down the road to the entrance to the brick works.

I reached the friendly lights of a neighbouring town. How glad I was to see them. I needed encouragement and human company. I went to a hotel where I was well known to the residents' lounge. The hall porter was remarkable for never saying a word that wasn't necessary. Once somebody asked him, "How did you propose to your wife?" He replied, "She did!" He came in with his tray, and looked at me to say, "Are you alright, Sir?" I said, "Yes." I ordered some whisky. Before he brought it the manageress came in to see if the fire was alright. In reality she came in to see if I was alright. She decided that I looked a bit worn but capable of travel and the hall porter brought me the whisky. I asked him to put it on the table because my hands were shaking. Somehow or other I never drank the whisky but drove home and went to bed.

I remember nothing more until I wakened up. There was the doctor and a lay brother. I heard the doctor say, "Well he has no temperature and his pulse is alright and there can be no real injury, but let us have a look. It was then I brushed aside his stethoscope. He said, "What happened to you?" I replied, "I saw the devil." Now, he was a North of Ireland man and I was Southern Irish and that was enough. "Well, well, well!"

He turned me over a couple of times, then he sent for some hot milk and into it he put the ends of a bottle of brandy. Along with that he gave me some pills and I settled down to sleep again. I had already slept for forty hours but I went off again into the sleep of the blessed.

About five o'clock the next morning I wakened up. I didn't know what time of day it was, I didn't know if it was morning or evening, but I had a terrible hunger.

There was then in our parish a devoted convert from the Salvation Army, and every Sunday she donated a steak and kidney pie with four hard-boiled eggs in the four corners of the dish. We were supposed to have it hot on Sunday, cold on Monday, and then make a sort of repast of it to end up. I was so hungry that I went downstairs and found a quarter of the cold steak and kidney pie with the hard boiled egg in the corner. I ate the lot.

The days went by. Then I found out that the devil never forgets, that he doesn't play fair, that he just doesn't observe the rules of the game. By the time I got rid of that steak and kidney pie I knew that devils are resisted by prayers and fasting, but never steak and kidney pie.

It is now more than thirty years ago. Brother Franco is dead, the doctor is dead, the hall porter is dead, she is dead and I am nearly dead. May God have mercy on all our souls!

There is a lesson in this story. Never invite the devil to meet you half way because he will come a little further. Don't try to peer into the future because God doesn't wish it. Don't try to look beyond the curtain of eternity because God has closed it forever. Don't try to double-cross God by invoking the aid of witches, necromancers, fortune-tellers and deluders. Those who practice the arts of spiritualism and witchery are quacks, but there is a small percentage who are really in the control of the devil and who have relations with him. If you meet him you are lost. He who sups with the devil needs a long spoon.

The swallows are here again

The swallows are back again. The last time I saw them they were lined up upon the telephone wires that cross the garden preparing to fly to North Africa. A long, long journey depending on where they are, depending on the point to which they return; maybe 2,000 miles. They looked almost twice as big as usual, they looked dirty. Now I know the reason why. They have to live and feed themselves on that journey to the South, so weeks before they depart they fly through the air catching as many insects as they can and storing them beneath their feathers and feed themselves upon the wing. Of course they look dirty before they go away but by the time they arrive the first thing they will need is a bath and that is why they will settle near water and mud. Water in which to wash themselves and mud from which they can construct their little houses.

161

Some of the young ones, still impudent, tear around wasting their energies, but the old ones sit quiet because they know they are in for something. They will not fly over the sea, they will skirt it, flying upon the thermal up-draughts that come from the mountains in the fading autumn sunlight. Sometimes they have a clear way, sometimes they meet with disastrous winds that beat them down and then they seek light and refuge and that is why occasionally thousands of them crash into lighthouses, to the comfort of the sheltering light. They are not hungry; if there is one thing they need it is a little warmth and shelter from the wind, a little time to rest.

Many of them will beat themselves to death against the lights, blinded by its brilliance, but only a percentage; the great majority escape. Lighthouse keepers can pick them up in their hands and stroke them and all they need to revive them is heat and shelter, then when the winds have died down they fly off again.

So it goes on, year by year, and it would go on until eternity; but now the insects in the air are poisoned by insecticide, swallows catch the insects and are poisoned themselves. These little gentlemen of the air are slowly being destroyed by the scientists. I wonder if there is such a thing as a scientific conscience. If I was a scientist and invented some pesticide that would ultimately destroy the swallows I would be sorry all my life.

Birds have always been the teachers of men. It is from the birds that men have learned to fly and by the study of their flight the dynamics of the air.

There is a new tunnel under Mont Blanc in the Alps – that chunk of rock is nearly 16,000 feet high and the tunnel enters the mountain between 3,000 and 4,000 feet up. It is 11.6 kilometres long and it is one of the most beautiful engineering feats in tunnel history. The tunnel connects France and Italy. The French worked from their end and the Italians from the other, and the two gangs met beneath the mountain and there was not an eighth of an inch difference in their calculations. It was so accurate that they had to make a line upon the wall to mark the point where the opposite teams met.

Naturally there was great jubilation and there was a lot of cleaning up to be done; but imagine the astonishment of the tunnel gangs when less than forty-eight hours after the tunnel was opened, birds were migrating through both from north and south. Moreover they were observing the traffic laws. Those going south kept to the right and those going north to the left. This is a remarkable instance of bird instinct and behaviour; how did the birds know there was a tunnel? How did they know instead of flying over Mont Blanc that they could fly under it? If an aeroplane tried to do the same thing it would have to acquire immense altitude in order to fly over the crest, and so indeed would the birds. How did they know that they could fly at a very low altitude and yet get through? We have a lot to learn.

Elias Lynch

163

The Carmelite Family in Britain

The Carmelite Family is one of the ancient religious communities of the Roman Catholic Church. Known officially as the *Brothers of the Blessed Virgin Mary of Mount Carmel*, the Carmelite Order developed from a group of hermits in thirteenth-century Palestine; priests and lay people living a contemplative life modelled on the prophet Elijah and the Virgin Mary. By the year 1214 the Carmelites had received a *Way of Life* from Saint Albert, the Latin Patriarch of Jerusalem. Carmelites first came to Britain in 1242. The hermits became an order of mendicant friars following a General Chapter held in Aylesford, Kent, in 1247. Nuns, and lay men and women have always played a major part in the life of the Order, and have had formal participation since 1452. Over centuries of development and reform, the Carmelites have continued their distinctive mission of living 'in allegiance to Jesus Christ', by forming praying communities at the service of all God's people. The heart of the Carmelite vocation is contemplation, that is, pondering God and God's will in our lives.

Like the spirituality of all the major religious orders (Benedictines, Franciscans, etc.), Carmelite spirituality is a distinct preaching of the one Christian message. Carmelites blend prayerful contemplation with active service of those around them, and this takes many different forms depending on the time and the place they find themselves in. Over the centuries 'Carmel' has produced some of the greatest Christian thinkers, mystics, and philosophers, such as Teresa of Jesus (of Avila), John of the Cross, and Thérèse of Lisieux (three Carmelite 'Doctors of the Church'). In the twentieth century, the Carmelite Family bore witness to the Gospel in the martyrdoms of Titus Brandsma, Edith Stein, and Isidore Bakanja.

England boasted the largest Carmelite Province in the Order until its suppression at the Reformation. The British Province was re-established under the patronage of Our Lady of the Assumption in the twentieth century. There are communities of friars, sisters and lay Carmelites across England,

Scotland, and Wales. Similar communities exist in Ireland, and throughout the world. The international Order of Discalced Carmelite friars, nuns, and laity is also present in Britain and Ireland. Members of the Carmelite and Discalced Carmelite Orders work, live, and pray together to make up the wider 'Carmelite Family', which seeks the face of the Living God in parishes, prisons, university chaplaincies, retreat centres, workplaces, schools, and through many other forms of ministry.

Further sources of information on Carmelite spirituality include:

John Welch, O.Carm.,
The Carmelite Way: An Ancient Path for Today's Pilgrim,
(Leominster: Gracewing, 1996).

Wilfrid McGreal, O.Carm.,
At the Fountain of Elijah: The Carmelite Tradition,
(London: Darton, Longman and Todd, 1999).

Website of the British Province of Carmelites
www.carmelite.org

165

The National Shrine of Saint Jude at Faversham

For more information:

The Church of Our Lady of Mount Carmel and the Shrine of St. Jude, Whitefriars, Faversham, Kent
(Faversham: Saint Albert's Press, 2004).

Website of the National Shrine of Saint Jude
www.stjudeshrine.org.uk

Website of the Parish of Our Lady of Mount Carmel, Faversham
www.whitefriarsfaversham.org

Write to:

St. Jude's Newsletter Office
Carmelite Friars
P. O. Box 140
Kent
ME20 7SJ
United Kingdom

Carmel on the web

The British Province of Carmelites
www.carmelite.org

National Shrine of Saint Jude, Faversham
www.stjudeshrine.org.uk

Parish of Our Lady of Mount Carmel, Faversham
www.whitefriarsfaversham.org

Aylesford Priory, Kent
www.thefriars.org.uk

Lay Carmel in Britain
www.laycarmel.org

Corpus Christi Carmelite Sisters
www.corpuschristicarmelites.org

Discalced Carmelite Family in England, Scotland & Wales
www.carmelite.org.uk

Irish Province of Carmelites
www.carmelites.ie

Anglo-Irish Province of Discalced Carmelites
www.ocd.ie

Association of Discalced Carmelite Nuns in Great Britain
www.carmelnuns.org.uk

Carmelite Forum of Britain and Ireland
www.carmeliteforum.org

Carmelite Institute of Britain and Ireland
www.cibi.ie

International Carmelite Index
www.carmelites.info

The Carmelite General Curia
www.ocarm.org

CITOC – Carmelite Communications Office
www.carmelites.info/citoc

Carmelite N.G.O. at the United Nations
www.carmelites.info/ngo

Edizioni Carmelitane
www.carmelites.info/edizioni

Domus Carmelitana, Rome
www.domuscarmelitana.com

167

Titles on Carmelite spirituality and history can be ordered from:

The Friars Bookshop
The Friars
Aylesford
Kent
ME20 7BX
U.K.

☎ + 44 (01622) 715770

E-mail:
bookshop@thefriars.org.uk

Saint Albert's Press
Book Distribution
Carmelite Friars
P.O. Box 140
ME20 7SJ
U.K.

☎ + 44 (01795) 537038

E-mail:
saintalbertspress@carmelites.org.uk

http://www.carmelite.org

LAUS DEO SEMPER ET MARIAE